"Dr. Budziszewski shoots straights when it comes to telling the Christian student about the challenges to one's faith that he or she can expect to encounter….Every church should give this book to their high school seniors who are headed to a college or university because such institutions can be a war zone for Christian students."

DEAN HALVERSON, General Editor of
The Compact Guide to World Religions

"The very existence of this book assumes and testifies to reality—the battle lines have been clearly drawn against the Christian in the academy….This book is pragmatic, honest, straight-shooting, biblically faithful, emphatically written, and soundly reasoned. Every serious Christian college student needs this book as a desktop reference next to the Bible."

DAVID C. NESS, Ph.D. Anthropology,
ministry consultant to university faculty

How to Stay Christian in College

An Interactive Guide to Keeping the Faith

J. Budziszewski

NAVPRESS

BRINGING TRUTH TO LIFE

P.O. Box 35001, Colorado Springs, Colorado 80935

The Navigators is an international Christian organization. Our mission is to reach, disciple, and equip people to know Christ and to make Him known through successive generations. We envision multitudes of diverse people in the United States and every other nation who have a passionate love for Christ, live a lifestyle of sharing Christ's love, and multiply spiritual laborers among those without Christ.

NavPress is the publishing ministry of The Navigators. NavPress publications help believers learn biblical truth and apply what they learn to their lives and ministries. Our mission is to stimulate spiritual formation among our readers.

Library of Congress Catalog Card Number: 98-49095

ISBN 1-57683-061-6

Cover: Sea Bird in Flight by Jana Leon/Graphistock

Some of the anecdotal illustrations in this book are true to life and are included with the permission of the persons involved. All other illustrations are composites of real situations, and any resemblance to people living or dead is coincidental.

Budziszewski, J., 1952-
    How to stay Christian in college : an interactive guide to keeping the faith / by J. Budziszewski.
        p. cm.
    Includes bibliographical references.
    ISBN 1-57683-061-6
    1. Christian college students—Religious life.   2. Christian college students—Conduct of life.   I. Title.
BV4531.2.B83 1999   98-49095
248.8'34—dc21   CIP

Unless otherwise identified, all Scripture quotations in this publication are taken from the *HOLY BIBLE: NEW INTERNATIONAL VERSION* ® (NIV®). Copyright © 1973, 1978, 1984 by International Bible Society. Used by permission of Zondervan Publishing House. All rights reserved. The other version included is the *Revised Standard Version Bible* (RSV), copyright © 1946, 1952, 1971, by the Division of Christian Education of the National Council of the Churches of Christ in the USA, used by permission, all rights reserved.

Printed in the United States of America

2 3 4 5 6 7 8 9 10 11 12 13 14 15 / 05 04 03 02 01 00 99

To my students

For my Lord

TABLE OF CONTENTS

How to Cope

Conclusion

ACKNOWLEDGMENTS

Heart's thanks are due to my wife and helpmate, Sandra, who helped me "think up" this book and serves as my best consultant; my daughter Alexandra, who finished high school just as I finished writing it and provided many details and advice; and my daughter Anastasia, who is still in college and checked all my claims against her own experience.

I'm deeply grateful for the encouragement of my good friends and yokemates in Austin, Robert Koons, Dave Geisler, and Dave Ness, respectively of the Department of Philosophy, University of Texas at Austin; Grad Resources, a campus student ministry; and Christian Leadership Ministries, an outreach to university faculty. Bill Dickson also lent his support electronically and by prayer.

Though I can't mention all the Christian students who have shared their questions, problems, thoughts, and survival stories with me over the years, special mention should be made of David Crockett, Matthew Furgiuele, Lynda Olman, Steven Barracca, and Michael Bailey. I'm confident that the names of the others are written in heaven. Some stories even came to me by E-mail, thanks to the efforts of Michael Sorgius, a Christian Leadership Ministries representative in Gainesville, Florida, and Marvin Olasky, of the Department of Journalism, University of Texas at Austin.

Brad Lewis deserves special mention for his editorial support and diligence, and I gladly render it.

I've written about some of the subjects in this book before, and I'd be a heel not to thank the journals in which these thoughts have appeared. My own story, in chapter 1, is condensed from a talk which has previously been published at greater length in *Real Issue* and in *Re:Generation Quarterly*, and which will also appear in *The Revenge of Conscience,* forthcoming in late 1999 from Spence Publishing. Several paragraphs of chapter 4 have been borrowed with only slight changes from "Opening Your Neighbors' Eyes," *Citizen,* Vol. 12, No. 1 (January 1998), and "What We Can't Not Know," *Human Life Review,* Vol. 22, No. 4 (Fall 1996). Chapter 7 adapts ideas that are much more fully expressed in "The Problem with Liberalism" and "The Problem with Conservatism," *First Things: A Monthly Journal of Religion and Public Life,* Nos. 61 and 62 (March and April 1996). Because *First Things* is online, anyone who would like to see the full text of the liberalism and conservatism articles can find them at http://www.firstthings.com.

My deepest debt is to my Lord Jesus Christ, who found me sixteen years ago in the Enemy's camp and gave me a new heart and mind.

INTRODUCTION

Chapter 1

College As Another World

Why Is This Book Necessary?

One day a student approached me after class. She seemed to be close to tears. "In lecture today, you mentioned that you're a Christian," she said. "I've never heard that from any other professor, and every day I spend at this university I feel my faith is under attack."

I knew just how she felt. Modern institutions of higher learning have changed dramatically in the last half-century, and from the moment students set foot on the contemporary campus their Christian convictions and discipline are assaulted. "Faith is just a crutch," they hear from friends and teachers. "The Bible is just mythology." "Christianity is judgmental and intolerant." "Morality is different everywhere." "Everyone must find his own truth." "I can be good without God." "Jesus was just a man who died." No wonder so many lose their faith! Soon after my own entrance into college I lost my faith myself, and I didn't find my way back to Jesus Christ until ten years later. This experience, along with seventeen years of teaching, has given me a heart for the struggles of all Christian students on the modern campus.

But here's the good news: Higher education doesn't have to be a wasteland. With a little help, Christian students can find college a means of God's blessing instead of a spiritual snare. Thousands do. In fact, during their college years, thousands of students rediscover Christ or find Him for the first time.

That's my wish for you.

My Own Story

Eighteen years ago, I stood before the Government Department at the University of Texas to give my here's-why-you-should-hire-me lecture. Fresh out of grad school, I wanted to teach about ethics and politics, so I was showing the faculty my stuff. What did I tell them? First, that we human beings just make up the difference between good and evil; second, that we aren't responsible for what we do anyway. For that, I was hired to teach.

I hadn't always believed these things. At the age of ten I had committed my life to Jesus Christ and was baptized. As a teenager I had not been a mature believer, but I had certainly been an enthusiastic one. Why had I fallen away from faith? For many reasons. One was that I had been caught up in the radical politics popular among many students in the late sixties and early seventies. I had my own ideas about redeeming the world, and my politics became a kind of substitute religion. During my student years I had also committed certain sins that I didn't want to repent. Because the presence of God made me more and more uncomfortable, I began looking for reasons to believe that He didn't exist. Then again, once I lost hold of God, things started going wrong in my life, and disbelieving in Him seemed a good way to get back at Him. Now of course if God didn't exist, then I couldn't get back at Him, so this may seem a strange sort of disbelief. But most disbelief is like that.

Another reason I lost my faith was that I'd heard all through school that human beings had created God in their image, and that even the most basic ideas about good and evil are arbitrary. During graduate school I had fallen under the spell of the nineteenth-century German writer Friedrich Nietzsche, the originator of the slogan "God is dead." If anything, I was more Nietzschean than Nietzsche. Whereas he thought that given the meaninglessness of things, nothing was left but to laugh or be silent, I recognized that not even laughter or silence was left. One had no reason to do or not do anything at all. This is a terrible thing to believe, but like Nietzsche, I imagined myself one of the few who could believe such things—who could walk the rocky heights where the air is thin and cold.

All of this gives you a clue to the main reason I lost faith in God: sheer, mulish pride. I didn't want God to be God; I wanted J. Budziszewski to be God. I see that now. But I didn't see that then.

Cool Webzine

Christians at college now have their own World Wide Web magazine. *Boundless* **is about everything from movies to dating to Deep Stuff, and there's even a monthly column by Yours Truly. Check out** *Boundless* **at http://www.boundless.org.**

I now believe that without God, everything goes wrong. This is true even of the good things He's given us, such as our minds. One of the good things I've been given is a stronger than average mind. I don't make the observation to boast; human beings are given diverse gifts to serve Him in diverse ways. The problem is that a strong mind refusing the call to serve God has its own way of going wrong. When some people flee from God they might rob and kill. When others flee from God they may do a lot of drugs and have a lot of sex. When I fled from God I didn't do any of those things; my way of fleeing was to get stupid. Though it always comes as a surprise to intellectuals, there are some forms of stupidity that you must be highly intelligent and educated to commit. God keeps them in his arsenal to pull down mulish pride, and I discovered them all.

More Alone Than I Thought

When I entered college I did not know what to expect. I was alone, I discovered, more alone than I thought [I would be]. At first my roommate and I got along, but that lasted about two weeks. Then I began to get more and more frustrated. I had left a boyfriend in California, and that complicated things.

—Anonymous college student

It was agony. You can't imagine what a person has to do to himself—well, if you're like I was, perhaps you can—what a person has to do to himself to go on believing the sort of nonsense I believed to shut out belief in the Gospel. Paul said that the knowledge of God's existence is plain from what He has made, and that the knowledge of his laws is "written on our hearts, our consciences also bearing witness." That means that so long as we have minds, we can't not know these things. Well, I was unusually determined not to know them; therefore I had to destroy my mind. For instance, I loved my wife and children, but I was determined to regard this love as merely a subjective preference with no real and objective value. Visualize a man opening up the access panels of his mind and pulling out all the components that have God's image stamped on them. The problem is that they all have God's image stamped on them, so the man can never stop. No matter how much he pulls out, there's still more to pull. I was that man.

How then did God bring me back? I came, over time, to feel a greater and greater horror about myself—an overpowering sense that my condition was terribly wrong. Finally it occurred to me to wonder why I should feel horror if the difference between the wonderful and the horrible was just something we humans make up. I had to admit that there was a difference between the wonderful and the horrible after all. And that meant that there had to exist a wonderful, of which the horrible was the absence. So my walls of self-deception collapsed all at once.

That was when I became aware again of the Savior I had deserted during college. Astonishingly, though I had abandoned Him, He had never abandoned me. I now believe He drew me back to Himself just in time. There is a point of no return, and I was almost there. I said I had been pulling out one component after another, and I had nearly got to the motherboard.

The next few years after my conversion were like being in a dark attic—one I had been in for a long time, but in which shutter after shutter was being thrown back so that great shafts of light began to stream in and illuminate the dusty corners. I recovered whole memories, whole feelings, whole ways of understanding that I had blocked out. As I look back, I am in awe that God has permitted me to make any contribution to His kingdom at all. But He promises that if only the rebel turns to Jesus Christ in repentant faith, giving up claims of self-ownership and allowing this Jesus, this Christ, the run of the house, He will redeem everything there is in it. And He did.

Many of my students tell me they struggle with the same dark influences that I once felt in college. I hope that by writing this book I may encourage you to seek the light—better yet, to avoid the darkness altogether.

WHO THIS BOOK IS FOR

I've written this book for three groups of people. The first group is Christian students who plan to go to college. The second is Christian students who are there already. My goal is to prepare, equip, and encourage *you* to meet the spiritual challenges of college life. Few new college students are ready for them.

> ## Growing Through Trials
> **My first two years at college were probably some of the most stressful of my life, and I thought high school was stressful! But I also know that I have done the most growing emotionally, physically (dorm food = fattening), mentally, and most important spiritually, through the trials, the missing people, and the loneliness.**
> **—Anonymous college student**

The third group is the parents of students in the other two groups. My goal is to help *them* understand what you're going through in college so they can offer more effective spiritual support. Maybe they never went to college. Maybe they went but can't remember what it was like. Maybe they remember, but they've heard that college today is different than it was when they were there.

This chapter gives a quick first look at what to expect in college. We'll go into some of these matters more closely later on.

ALL ALONE

College means leaving many people behind and going into a world of strangers. If you know some of the people at your college already, you might think it won't be that way. For example, maybe some of your high school friends graduated a year ahead of you and went to the same college you're planning to attend. They were glad to hang around with you when they came home for summer break, so you're thinking they'll be glad to hang around with you when you show up on campus.

Things might work out that way, but they might not. Chances are your old friends will seem different on campus than they do in your hometown. For one thing, they'll probably be busier. For another, during their year at college they will have formed new interests that you don't share and joined new social circles where you're a stranger. They may be less interested in spending time with you than they were at home. Or they may be just as interested, but act differently than they did at home. You weren't expecting their new ways because during summer break they fell back into their old ones. Changes like these may make it hard to get your old footing back with them. You know them—*sure* you know them!—but somehow they're strangers too.

Another reason you might think "aloneness" won't be an issue is that some of your friends are going to college *with* you: they've graduated from high school at the same time and chosen the same college. But you may be surprised how this works out too. High school is a smaller world than college. At college there are more people, more groups, and more activities. There are also more things to learn and more opportunities to make mistakes. Sometimes old friends grow closer at college, but sometimes they grow apart. There's no way to predict what will happen in advance.

Top Ten Party Schools

Based on surveys by Princeton Review of 56,000 students concerning "the use of alcohol and drugs, hours of study each day, and the popularity of the Greek system," the top ten party schools are:

1. **State University of New York, Albany**
2. **University of Wisconsin, Madison**
3. **University of Florida, Gainesville**
4. **University of Georgia, Athens**
5. **University of Colorado, Boulder**
6. **Florida State University, Tallahassee**
7. **Ohio University, Athens**
8. **University of Kansas, Lawrence**
9. **University of Vermont, Burlington**
10. **Seton Hall University, South Orange, New Jersey**[1]

So one way or another, to one degree or another, aloneness will be an issue for you at college. Not everyone reacts to aloneness in the same way. For example, some feel lonely, while others don't (or say they don't). Whether lonely or not, everyone is affected *somehow* by aloneness, because we were designed to be with others. God said it wasn't good for Adam to be alone, and it isn't good for us either.

The important thing is to seek and build new interests and attachments in a careful, discerning way. You don't need to panic. College is full of social opportunities, and most students are more ready to form friendships than at any other time in their lives. This book devotes a whole chapter, and parts of several others, to campus social life.

SUDDENLY ADULT

If you were a typical teenager, you probably grumbled for years about the rules and limits your parents made you obey. Well, no one makes you obey them in college. Once upon a time, colleges and universities regarded themselves as standing *in loco parentis,* "in the place of the parents." Except at a few Christian colleges, that notion hasn't been taken seriously for years. Unless you cheat, commit a crime, or disrupt the campus, your school is unlikely to know—or even care—how you live. No one will tell you not to stay up so late. No one will wake you in the morning if you oversleep. No one will tell you when to come home from a date. No one will make you go to church. No one will remind you to do your homework, wash your underwear, or stay away from sex and drugs. In these ways, you are forced to take responsibility for your own behavior.

Being thrust all at once into the responsibilities of adulthood can come as a shock. Some of my students visit me to seek advice about life after graduation. Many have made poor grades right up until their senior year. I ask them why. "When I got to the university I went wild," says one. "For my first three years here I just partied," says another. "Do you think that will hurt my chances of getting into law school?" You can guess how I have to answer.

People invent all sorts of ways to adapt to the sudden pressure of adult responsibility. Some ways help, others don't. When I started college, one of the guys in the dorm told me that he'd found the perfect way to motivate himself to study. He kept an enormous jug of a cheap fruit-flavored wine on his desk, and for each page of homework he read, he rewarded himself with a swallow. As you might guess, he was always a little drunk. He got his reading done, but whether he remembered what he'd read was another question. I don't remember seeing him take notes either. Maybe he couldn't hold the pencil!

College sends students mixed messages. Although in some ways it treats them as grownups, in other ways it treats them as babies. You don't have to prepare your own meals, because you can eat in the cafeteria. You don't have to find your own doctor, because you can go to the student health clinic. You don't have to come up with your own entertainment, because music, movies, and other amusements are provided on most campuses. If you live in the dorm you might not even have to launder your own sheets, because a maid brings fresh ones every week. All sorts of things are done for you at college that you're perfectly capable of doing for yourself. The arrangement has some advantages, but it hardly encourages you to remember that you're grown up.

Of course you *really are* grown up in one sense (you have full adult responsibilities) even though you *really aren't* grown up in another (you haven't finished developing). What kind of person are you going to become? I'm not talking about the courses you want to take or the kind of job you want to get someday; I'm talking about the qualities you want to have. Do you desire to be wise, fair, and honest—or foolish, unfair, and crooked? Kind, loyal, and reliable—or mean, backstabbing, and unreliable? Brave, faithful, and pure—or cowardly, weak, and stained? Maybe you've thought about the kind of person you want to become, but not about how to become that person. Every act, every decision, every thought will move you either a little closer to being that kind of person—or push you a little further away.

What are the small temptations in your life? To become reliable in the big things, you have to practice reliability in the small ones. To become pure in the big things, you have to practice purity in the small ones. If you haven't started practicing yet, now is the time. Pray for strength and begin.

On Another Planet

Going to college can be like moving to Mars. The first change you'll notice will be in your physical surroundings. If you're used to seeing cornfields stretching all the way to the horizon, and your college is in the city where you can't see the horizon at all, the landscape may come as a shock. If you're used to getting everywhere by subway and bus, and your college is in a spread-out place where there's no public transportation and you have to drive, the change may be hard to get used to—especially if you don't have a car!

Compared to the cultural difference, though, the difference in your physical surroundings will seem tiny. People at college may talk differently, socialize differently, and even eat differently. One reason for cultural differences, of course, is change in region, and the farther from home you go to school, the greater such differences are likely to be. They may be hard to take. Southerners, unused to the hurry and crowding of Northeastern cities, tend to consider Northeasterners rude and unfriendly. Northeasterners, unused to the relaxed speech and elaborate courtesy of the South, sometimes think Southerners are slow and stupid. It isn't always easy for such different groups to understand each other.

An even bigger reason college may seem like Mars is the culture of the campus itself. Each school tends to develop a personality of its own. Some have good personalities; others don't. The personality of the school one friend attended for his first two years was neurotically intense and competitive. He'll never forget one of the talks given during Freshman Orientation. The speaker, a dean, dwelled upon the large number of freshman at the school who committed suicide or received psychological counseling. He wasn't warning them—he was *bragging,* because he thought suicidal tendencies were a proof of intellectual brilliance! By contrast, the college another friend attended turned out to be a "party school." In her dorm, the floors used to organize Progressive Drinking Nights. Students who participated went from room to room getting drunker and drunker. A number of women in the dorm announced that on certain evenings, they would have sex with any men who showed up at their doors. So many men showed up that they had to form lines. By the way, don't assume that your college will have a Christian personality just because it's linked with a Christian denomination, says Christian things in its mission statement, or has the word "Christian" in its name. There's more Christianity at some nonChristian schools than at some so-called Christian schools.

A final reason for feeling that you've landed on another planet is that colleges and universities are magnets for extreme beliefs, ideologies, and cults. At one school recently, campus feminists protested sex discrimination by marching into town topless. (Take *that,* you sexists!) At another, homosexuals sponsored an outdoor gay "kiss-in" to win acceptance for their cause. I know of an art professor who lists on her résumé that she tied herself to another artist with a rope for a year. (She says they never touched.) Another professor, this one in the social sciences, offers a course every year on creating your own reality. (He says it's very practical.) I'm not making this stuff up.

The sheer weirdness of the new environment puts some students into what sociologists call "culture shock"—taking the weirdness too hard and becoming deeply homesick and depressed. At the other extreme, some students adapt by "going native"—losing their sense of who they are and plunging into the ways of the people around them.

Four simple tips will help you keep your feet on the ground.

1. Research the school's personality ahead of time to make sure you're choosing a good one.
2. Remember that it's *normal* to feel somewhat odd and homesick in any new place and that such feelings normally pass.
3. Remember that a little worldly homesickness can be spiritually good for you. It's a reminder that Christians are *always* strangers in this world, for we are citizens of heaven.
4. Keep up your spiritual disciplines. What I mean is daily prayer, frequent Bible study and worship, evangelism, service to others, and constantly reminding yourself of the presence of God. If you stay focused on Christ, He'll make even the desert bloom.

Seven Things to Do About Mild Homesickness

1. **Pray**
2. **Call home**
3. **Write a letter**
4. **Do something with a friend**
5. **Help out in a volunteer service project**
6. **Get together with your Christian fellowship group**
7. **Have a good cry, then find something constructive to do**

UNDER PRESSURE

Think back to the student I mentioned at the beginning of the chapter who told me that every day she spent at the university she felt that her faith was under attack.

The early Christians risked death and torture for their faith. Some were crucified, others beheaded. Still others were roasted, shot with arrows, or thrown to wild beasts. A Roman emperor, Caligula, burned them to light up his garden parties. In various countries, Christians still suffer torture for Christ. In fact, historians of the faith say there have been more martyrs in our century than in all of the previous centuries put together. Thousands are also sold into slavery or sent to "reeducation" camps. Yet the cause of Christ continues to spread.

Was my student under *that* kind of attack? No. She was merely in an atmosphere that made Christian faith look ridiculous. Was that all? Yes. And is that kind of thing enough to explain why the modern university has reverted to paganism? Apparently so!

How can this be?

The answer isn't hard to understand. Violent persecution focuses the mind on the fact that the kingdom of this world is an enemy to the kingdom of God. When there hasn't been any persecution for a long time—as in our part of the world—many Christians start expecting the world to be a friend. They slip into seeking the world's approval instead of God's. When the world *denies* its approval—when the teacher smirks or some of the other students roll their eyes—they go hollow inside.

How can you stand firm? I'm sure you aren't surprised when I tell you again to keep up the Christian disciplines. Spend time with God in prayer, study His Word, tell others about Him, and show mercy to those in need. But it's hard to do that all by yourself, isn't it? I have good news for you. God has not left you all by yourself. He provided the church. You need to seek out your partners in the faith and have frequent fellowship with them. Pray and study and show mercy, yes, but don't do it just by yourself; do it with your brothers and sisters in Christ. You see, God made us social beings; that's why we respond so readily to peer pressure. Peer pressure is good if it's the right kind of pressure from the right kind of peers. Your true peer group is the fellowship of the saints, the household of God.

> ## "This, Above All Others, Has Been the Century of Christian Martyrdom." —Richard John Neuhaus[2]
>
> **More Christians have been martyred in this century than in all previous centuries put together. Around the world, some 300,000 are put to death annually for their faith. Some of the organizations that help persecuted Christians are International Christian Concern, Shatter the Silence, and Voice of the Martyrs.**

This is a great secret. I don't mean that God hides it; I mean not many Christian students know it. They try to live their faith alone and find themselves losing heart. No wonder! That's not the way God planned it.

Everyone has had conversations he wishes he could have over again. I now realize that the student who spoke to me about being under attack hadn't yet discovered the secret I've just told you. I wish I could speak with her again so I could tell her. There's no such thing as a solitary Christian. If you go into the world alone, you'll be swallowed.

How This Book Can Help

You can use this book in three ways. First, you can read it straight through. If you haven't reached college yet, don't worry if not everything you read "clicks" right away, because some parts will make better sense after you get to college and see for yourself what I'm talking about.

Second, you can take this book along to college and use it as a handbook. As you run into the kinds of problems and situations I write about, you can return to the chapters that cover them.

Third, you can share the book with friends. Didn't I just say that there's no such thing as a solitary Christian? You need them, but they need you too.

The apostle Paul said, "Do not be conformed to this world but be transformed by the renewal of your mind" (Romans 12:2, RSV). I see this verse as a charter for Christian students. To help you renew your mind, the next three chapters help you understand how others see life.

Chapter 2 is *What God Thinks of the World.* The understanding of Jesus you gained as a child is precious to God but may not be enough to survive the challenges of college; as a young adult, you need meat as well as milk. This chapter is a more mature presentation of what the good news is all about—man's sin and God's response.

Chapter 3 is *What the World Thinks of Itself.* The modern university is profoundly alienated from God and hostile to Christian faith, so in order to stay centered in the gospel you need to learn about the nonChristian worldviews commonly met on campus. That's what this chapter is for.

Chapter 4 is *Talking with NonChristian Friends.* NonChristians and wavering Christians offer numerous objections to the Christian life and worldview. This chapter explains how to talk to both groups—and what to say once you've started.

Paul also said, "Examine yourselves to see whether you are in the faith; test yourselves. Do you not realize that Christ Jesus is in you—unless, of course, you fail the test?" (2 Corinthians 13:5). To help you test yourself and keep free from delusions, Part II of the book is about *Campus Myths.*

Chapter 5 is *Myths About the Search for Knowledge.* False ideas about the relationship between faith and reason undermine the confidence of many college Christians and encourage other students to be hostile to Christianity. This chapter sets the record straight by explaining how faith and reason are *really* related.

Chapter 6 is *Myths About Love and Sex.* False ideas about love and sex make some college Christians wonder whether sexual purity is worth the trouble. It is, and in this chapter you learn what sexual purity is all about.

Chapter 7 is *Myths About Politics.* Passionate secular political ideologies yank some college Christians away from their identity in Christ. This chapter is where you find out where nonChristian elements are hidden in the thinking of both Left and Right political ideologies.

To flourish as a Christian you need to know how to put all these things into practice, so the last major part of the book is about *How to Cope.*

Chapter 8 is *Coping in Campus Social Life.* Campus social life will pose special challenges for you because it doesn't conform to a Christian pattern. In this chapter we talk about how to be faithful in friendship, fun, and dating.

Chapter 9 is *Coping in Campus Religious Life.* As I explained earlier, living the faith requires mutual support among believers; the problem is that not every campus "Christian" group lives up to its name. This chapter explains how to find a healthy and faithful Christian fellowship.

Chapter 10 is *Coping in the Classroom.* Although Christians have plenty to learn in college, the classroom can sometimes be intimidating. The goal of this chapter is to show you how to practice intellectual discernment, how to hold your own in a discussion, and how to deal with classmates and professors who think Christians must be stupid.

In the *Conclusion* of the book, chapter 11, we'll talk about *The Meaning of Your Life.* God aims at more than making you live forever; His goal is to make each Christian a mirror of His joy and glory. Nothing happens by chance, and if He has put you in college, He has a reason for your being there. The more fully you understand this reason, the more perfectly you can serve and enjoy Him.

WORLDVIEWS

Chapter 2

WHAT GOD THINKS OF THE WORLD

You've probably never thought about it, but Sunday school teachers face a dilemma. Children love to hear about Jesus, and they ask searching questions. But you have to keep the answers simple or kids become confused. Teenagers want to know about God too—and they can understand deeper answers—but getting all those hormones to listen is another matter. What's the result? As students grow older, the intellectual level of their Christian training often *drops* instead of rises! Many of them never get beyond a child's understanding of the faith. They carry it right into college, where it's all too often blown away.

When Jesus said you have to enter the kingdom like a child, He meant you have to enter with a child's trust, not with a child's understanding. So I'm going to level with you. This chapter presents the basics of the Christian faith all over again—but at an adult level. If you're not typical and have a great deal of knowledge about your faith, great! But you may want to read this chapter anyway.

Cults

A great resource on groups that look Christian but aren't is the Christian Research Institute and its magazine, the *Christian Research Journal*. You can E-mail questions to CRI from the web page http://www.equip.org/free.htm.

Hundreds of articles from *Christian Research Journal* and other Christian magazines are archived by the Institute for Christian Leadership. To read them, visit the web page http://www.iclnet.org/search.html. Just type in the name of the cult you want to know about, then click "search" or "go."

For another solid resource, check out the cults page of Probe Ministries at http://www.probe.org/menus/wp-cults.html.

My main goal is clarity, so I'm going to be direct. Many cults take Christian words and pour nonChristian meanings into them, so I want you to be able to detect when that's happening. Let's get going.

GOD

God is like nothing we could have imagined.

God is utterly *other* than us—other in a way we express with the word *holiness.* Yes, He dwells within each Christian, but He's *not you.* He isn't the same as you, He isn't a part of you, and He isn't a "higher" you. Yes, you're made in His image, but you're *not Him.* You're not the same as Him, you're not a part of Him, and you aren't a "splinter" of Him. Nor will you ever be. He doesn't depend on anything else because He is what everything else depends on. He can't be explained by anything else because He is what everything else must be explained by. Although we can know what He has taught us about Himself, we can never comprehend Him completely because He is greater than our minds. Anything He wills, He can do. He not only holds supreme power, He also uses it. Nothing can defeat Him and nothing can happen contrary to His will. He is also supremely good—light with no darkness. Although evil is real, He detests it and brings it to judgment. He knows everything, He pays attention to everything, and nothing escapes His notice. He's not just a *What* and a *Who,* like me or like you, but one *What* in three *Whos*—one God in three Persons: Father, Son, and Holy Spirit.[1] There is no one like Him. He is set apart. He is what He is, and there was never a time when He was not.

Do you want to know what God's holiness means? Then meditate awhile on these incidents. When Moses asked God what he should tell the people God's name was, God said, "Tell them my name is I Am." Then when Moses asked to see God face to face, God said no, because it would kill Moses. When Isaiah caught just a glimpse of the glory of God, he said, "Woe is me! I am undone." When the glory of God came into the ancient temple, strong men fell down. When the High Priest went into the Most Holy Place of the ancient temple, he went with a linen rope tied onto his ankle, so that if he didn't survive the nearness of God, the other priests who stayed outside could pull out his body.

On the other hand God is utterly *intimate* with us—intimate in a way we express with the word *love.* He's our father. He's our master. He's our brother. He's our shepherd. He's our husband. He's our friend. If you think these are "just figures of speech," that's fine. But remember that figures of speech are always mere shadows of the real thing.

God's Love

By day the LORD directs his love,
at night his song is with me—
a prayer to the God of my life.

—Psalm 42:8

Because your love is better than life,
my lips will glorify you.

—Psalm 63:3

My son, do not despise the LORD's discipline
and do not resent his rebuke,
because the LORD disciplines those he loves,
as a father the son he delights in.

—Proverbs 3:11-12

You see, at just the right time, when we were still
powerless, Christ died for the ungodly. Very rarely
will anyone die for a righteous man, though for a
good man someone might possibly dare to die. But
God demonstrates his own love for us in this: While
we were still sinners, Christ died for us.

—Romans 5:6-8

Whoever does not love does not know God, because
God is love. This is how God showed his love among
us: He sent his one and only Son into the world that
we might live through him. This is love: not that we
loved God, but that he loved us and sent his Son as
an atoning sacrifice for our sins. . . . We love because
he first loved us.

—1 John 4:8-11,19

Do you want to know how God loves us? Then think awhile on these lines. This is God speaking to you: "Your lips drop sweetness as the honeycomb, my bride; milk and honey are under your tongue. The fragrance of your garments is like that of Lebanon. You are a garden locked up, my sister, my bride; you are a spring enclosed, a sealed fountain" (Song of Songs 4:11-12). Has He made His intentions clear?

I said before that God is like nothing we could have imagined. We could never have imagined His *holiness*. We could never have imagined His *love*. Even if we could, we could never have imagined them *together*. Haven't you noticed that when people get worked up about His holiness they sometimes forget His love, and when they get worked up about His love they sometimes forget His holiness? But that just shows that we don't understand either the holiness or the love.

Put that love and that holiness together and you get what you might be tempted to call a fanatic. Maybe you don't want God to be that holy. Maybe you don't want to be loved that much. Maybe you don't want to be loved that much *by* something that holy, for our God is a consuming fire. None of that makes a speck of difference to Him. Though we can reject His loving pursuit, God is relentless, inexorable, and utterly unfettered in His pursuit of us. He empties Himself, pours Himself out for us, to the point of death, whether we want Him to or not. He crushes our sin. He is utterly opposed to whatever in us opposes Him. He wants *us* to be holy, to be set apart *for Him*. And He expects us to like it! We are commanded—get that?—*commanded* to be joyful about it. What nerve.

The Bible is the story of *this* God's dealings with His people: From the beginning, down to the present, into the future, up to the end.

CREATION

When you were in kindergarten and drew a pink cat with blue wings, your teacher might have praised you by saying, "My, what a beautiful drawing you created." Such a compliment is too generous for human beings! People do come up with new things, of course, because God has given us imagination. But only one being can *create*, and that's God.

How is what we do different from what He does? Think back to that cat. What made your picture original was that you'd never seen a pink cat with blue wings. You made it up. But you didn't make it up *completely* because you'd seen cats before, you'd seen wings before, you'd seen pink before, and you'd seen blue before. We merely recombine old things in new ways; God makes up really new things from nothing. That's what it means to create. Only God actually creates.

You can mix blue and yellow to make green, but He invented color. You can have dessert before dinner instead of after, but He invented time. You can put the steeple on the side of the church instead of the top, but He invented place. He invented matter and energy, bodies and spirits, qualities and properties, everything there is. We only rearrange.

A student once told me he wanted to *create* his own morality. But we can't make up new moral laws; we can only keep or break the ones God has given us already. How could you turn a moral law false that had been true before? How could you turn a moral claim true that had been false before? Someone else said to me that parents *create* their children. But all parents can do is offer their bodies as an occasion for God's creativity. The father doesn't design the genes that he contributes. The mother doesn't design the genes that she contributes. Neither of them invented the sexual act that combines their genes, and neither of them invented the process that forms the baby. You may as well call it "creation" when a child mixes tea with sweetener to get sweetened tea.

Now let me tell you something surprising: God didn't have to create, and nothing made Him create. He wasn't lacking anything, and He didn't need anything. Some students think He must have been sitting around in the dark before creation, doing nothing and getting lonely. They think He created so that He would have someone to talk with, someone to know Him. That's a sub-Christian view of God. If the infinite God could be lonely, then His loneliness would be an infinite loneliness. Finite creatures like *us* couldn't take it away. But He wasn't lonely anyway. How could He be? Remember, He is tri-personal, one God in three Persons, one *What* in three *Whos*. You and I need others to be social, but He is social in His very nature. He keeps Himself the best company there is.

Does it hurt your feelings that God doesn't need you? Maybe you think this means He doesn't love you. No, you have it backward. It means He loves you even better than you thought. True, I might well suspect that my wife didn't love me if *she* said *she* didn't need me. But that's because human love can't be separated from need. We love not only to fulfill the needs of other people, but also to fulfill our own. And that's all right up to a point, because God made us full of needs. But His love isn't like ours. It's not need-love; it's pure gift-love. Though He needs nothing from us, He pours Himself out for us. Nothing drove Him to create us, yet He did.

Every religion has myths about origins, but only in the Bible do we find a picture of a *real* creation— an eternal Someone making up something out of nothing. According to all of the other religions, *stuff* merely develops into similar *stuff*, or perhaps remains unchanged. For instance some of them say the universe "gave rise" or "gave birth" to God. Others say some kind of god or god-stuff "gave rise" or "gave birth" to the universe. Still others say God and the universe are the *same,* or that one contains the other. You see that they don't really have an idea of creation, and that's why they can't really tell God apart from what He made. That's why they worship created things instead of the Creator Himself— whether a tribesman makes an idol of stone, a poet makes an idol of his feelings, or a wealthy man makes an idol of what he can buy. The Bible calls this sin.

So get this: God is distinct from His creation. He isn't a part of it; it isn't a part of Him. He didn't "arise" from it; it didn't "arise" from Him. He spoke, and where nothing was before, *it was.*

THE BAD NEWS

At first it's puzzling how there can be a Bad News, because everything God created is good. Some people think He created evil as well as good, or that a good god created all the good things like light, health, and virtue, and a bad god created all the bad ones like darkness, disease, and sin. But that doesn't make sense. Why not? Because evil isn't created—it isn't made up from nothing.

Where does it come from, then? The only way to get a bad thing is to take a good thing and spoil it. For example, darkness isn't made up from nothing; you get it by blocking the light. Disease isn't made up from nothing; you get it by ruining health. Notice that this doesn't work the other way around—you can't get light by blocking darkness or health by ruining disease. So God created only good things, but some of them have been spoiled. That's even true about Satan. He's just a created being—an angel who was made good but went bad. To be evil at all, Satan needs good things that he can abuse, things like intelligence, power, and will. Those good things come from God.

Now God chose to make us the chief good, the jewel, of His creation. He made us in His own image. That doesn't mean we're God—we've been through that already. It means we're little portraits of Him. Not of His looks—because God is a Spirit—but of His qualities. We were made to mirror the glory of His truth, to burn with the fire of His holiness, and most of all to flare with the flame of His love.

All this raises a question: If love is what God made us for, why didn't He make us so we *had to* love Him? Because there is no *had to* in loving. Love is a commitment of the will. If we had to love, it wouldn't be love. To be capable of loving God, we had to be capable of turning away from Him. And that's where the Bad News begins.

God was pleased with His work, but from earliest times, we've ruined it. We decided God could go fly a kite. Instead of being satisfied to be made in His image, we wanted to take His place. Genesis 3 tells how we came up with our own ideas about how to be "like gods," and we weren't willing to wait for His instruction. This rebellion is called sin. First it clawed us apart from God Himself. Then it soured the relationship between man and woman, brother and brother, nation and nation, and man and the created heavenly beings.

That's not all. It also ruined us inwardly because although we've pulled ourselves away from God, we were designed for harmony with Him. Because our minds no longer obey Him, our desires and emotions no longer obey our minds. Yes, by His mercy, some good things still exist in us. But not one of those good things is in its original healthy state; each has been fatally distorted. Even our best experiences, like love, are mixed with sin. Try going a week without selfishness, resentment, or lust. Try going a day. Try going an hour. You can't, unless something distracts you. Maybe not even then.

Love Without Limits

Praise the LORD, O my soul;
    all my inmost being, praise his holy name.
Praise the LORD, O my soul,
    and forget not all his benefits—
who forgives all your sins
    and heals all your diseases,
who redeems your life from the pit
    and crowns you with love and compassion,
who satisfies your desires with good things
    so that your youth is renewed like the eagle's.

The LORD is compassionate and gracious,
    slow to anger, abounding in love.
He will not always accuse,
    nor will he harbor his anger forever;
he does not treat us as our sins deserve
    or repay us according to our iniquities.
For as high as the heavens are above the earth,
    so great is his love for those who fear him;
as far as the east is from the west,
    so far has he removed our transgressions from us.
                    —Psalm 103:1-5,8-12

Not only are we ruined, but we can't repair ourselves. Could you perform surgery on your own eyes or treat yourself for madness? Suppose you tore off both arms; without your hands, could you sew them back on? Our sin-sickness is something like that. We may long to love purely, but the needs in our need-love have become idols that control us. We may long to be holy, but our righteousness has become self-righteousness that rules us. We may long to be reconciled with God, but we can't stop wanting to be the center of the universe ourselves.

Worst of all, we face judgment. A God whose love is inexorable must spurn whatever is contrary to His love. In spite of what some people want to think, there is such a thing as hell. Jesus, the very person who taught that God is love, warned more about hell than anyone else in the Bible. I have to be careful here, because some Christian preachers have overdone it by not talking about anything else, and anti-Christian writers have spread confusion by calling hell "cruel" and "sadistic." The important thing is to remember what hell and heaven really are. Heaven is a place and condition of perfect fellowship with God; hell is a place and condition of absolute separation from God.

Some writers have said that the flames of hell are not real flames but mere metaphors for the agony of being left to ourselves. I think this is probably true, but remember that a metaphor is just a shadow of the real thing; if flames are a mere metaphor for that agony, the agony must be worse than flames. Other writers have said that no one ends up in hell unless he *wants* to be left to himself. Again I think this is probably true, but isn't being left alone what we *all* want when we sin? In hell, God merely gives us what we've wanted all along, and He lets the horrible natural results of our choices take full effect! We hate it, but there's no place else we'd like better. Suppose He put us in heaven instead. (He wouldn't, because He won't have sin near Him, but let's pretend.) In our sinful condition, heaven itself would be hell to us. The very radiance of His love would make our skin peel.

By all human reckoning, then, the situation is hopeless. We are broken beyond the ability to fix ourselves, fallen beyond the strength to rise up. By our own rebellion we are separated by an infinite distance from our Creator, and we don't have the power to get back. Each of us has a seed of hell inside, and each day it grows a little bigger; short of a miracle, one day it will burst out and devour us. We cannot save ourselves.

Further Reading About Heaven and Hell
Both of these articles are by Rick Rood.

"The Truth about Heaven."[2] You can read it on the web at http://www.probe.org/docs/heaven.html.

"Is There Really a Hell?"[3] Check it out at http://www.probe.org/docs/hell.html.

The Good News

By all *human* reckoning the situation is hopeless, but not by God's. We can't save *ourselves,* but God can save us.

How? Can God just overlook our sin? Well, He *does* overlook it for a time—I mean He doesn't bring down His judgment on us all at once. But this doesn't solve our problem. We can't be reconciled with God and be His enemies at the same time, and we just don't know how to stop being His enemies. No one can stop sinning just by deciding never to sin.

Our problem has another side too: We're just plain guilty. Disloyalty to your family, your country, your friend, or your spouse is bad enough, but disloyalty to God is the worst thing in the universe. The worst thing carries the worst penalty. God would be less than just if it didn't.

Can't we just *pay* the penalty? Well, in one sense, yes, but in the important sense, no. The penalty for sin is death, and I don't just mean physical death but spiritual death—not only loss of life but loss of God. God made this penalty an automatic consequence of sin's deed, in just the same way that drowning is an automatic consequence of filling your lungs with water. I suppose that in a sense, unending death would pay the penalty for being unendingly in the wrong, but it wouldn't solve our problem, would it? The payment would never be over, and it would still leave us dead.

Could someone pay the death penalty *for* us, the way I might pay a money debt for someone who didn't have any money of his own? That's an interesting idea, but awfully difficult. Just think—what kind of person could pay our debt against God?

First, to pay our debt against God the payer would have to be capable of paying *that kind* of debt. He would have to be able to suffer a human death, and that means he would have to be a human being himself. The difficulty here is that death is just the problem we humans are trying to get away from.

Second, to pay our debt against God the payer would have to be capable of paying *that large* a debt. He would have to have infinite resources, because we've committed infinite offense against God. The difficulty here is that the only one who has infinite resources is God Himself.

Third, to pay our debt against God the payer would have to be able to *stand for other* human beings. He would have to share our human nature completely and be so perfectly one with us that what happened to him counted as happening to us. The difficulty here is that we had a representative once—the first man, Adam—but he blew it.

Fourth, to pay our debt against God the payer would have to be without any debt himself. He would have to be *sinless*—completely holy and in perfect fellowship with God. The difficulty here is that all of us have sinned.

Fifth, to pay our debt against God the payer would have to pay the debt *willingly*. He would have to sacrifice himself for us, to walk with his eyes open into the agony we've brought down on our heads. The difficulty here is that our love comes nowhere near the mark of a sacrifice like that.

To sum up these requirements, our debt against God could be paid only by a sinless human being who could count as a new representative of every human being, one who loved us so much that he was willing to spend himself for us—but who was also God, so that He could spend Himself without limit.

In other words, God Himself would have to take the heat for us.

As a man.

And He did it.

He who could pay the penalty but didn't deserve it, paid for us who deserved to pay but couldn't do it. God, still fully God, became fully man as well, so that He could pour Himself out on an executioner's cross as our representative. That's who Jesus was—both Son of God and Son of Man—and that's what Jesus did.

And there's more. Remember, we're not only guilty but also broken. That means we need not only forgiveness but fixing. We need to be not only made right with God but also transformed. Jesus took care of this problem too, because He not only died but also rose again. Just as our old life with its sin can be nailed with Him on the cross, so also we can be raised up with Him to eternal life with God. Somehow our guilt flows onto Him, and somehow His life flows into us. Through Him, we gradually become capable of living as

A Professor Shares His Faith

I'm a Christian not because I have been convinced by some impressive arguments: arguments from natural theology for the existence of God, historical arguments concerning the authenticity of the Scriptures or the reliability of the apostles, or whatever. My coming back was less like seeing that certain premises implied a conclusion than it was like coming to hear some things in music that I hadn't heard before, or having my eyes opened to the significance of things that are going on around me. G. K. Chesterton once wrote: "In the last analysis, the reason why I am a Christian is that the Church is living and not a dead teacher." That pretty much sums it up for me. I'm a Christian because it was in the Christian Church that I came to discover the presence and activity of God in my life.

—Professor William P. Alston, "Why I Am a Christian."[4]
You can read the rest of his testimony at
http://www.leaderu.com/truth/1truth23.html.

we could never live before—of obeying Him more profoundly than we ever did before.

Eternal life means not just living forever, but living forever with a new kind of life. It begins with the cancellation of the curse, but goes on to perfect holiness. It begins with the forgiveness of sins, but goes on to joy and glory. Think of salvation as being adopted into a family. The legal change, from outsider to son or daughter, takes place in just an instant. But slowly you grow up in your new family and come into the inheritance that your new Father has been holding for you all along.

The Good News, then, is that in Jesus, who died for our sins and rose to eternal life, God has made a path for us to get back to Him—a way for us to be forgiven, fixed, and finally glorified.

A Student Shares His Faith

It was as if God was knocking on the door of my heart…but I didn't want to let Him in. I kept thinking about how my life would change and how my friends would think I was weird. I was scared. But the more I thought about it, the more God helped me realize that entering into a relationship with Him was the right thing to do. So I told Him that I wanted Him to come into my life.

What happened next is difficult to describe. I can only put it this way: I "met" God. And when I met Him I discovered real fulfillment. I felt a wholeness I had never experienced before, as if an empty part of me deep down in my soul had been filled—a wholeness that has been a part of my life ever since that day.

My experience is not unique. It's what Jesus Christ offers to do in anyone's life.

—University of Texas student John Gay, "Where I Found Real Fulfillment."[5] You can read the rest of his testimony at http://www.leaderu.com/everystudent/reallife/reallife2.html.

YOU

You'll hear that there are many ways to God. God says different. Imagine that you're all alone at the bottom of a pit. The pit is miles deep but barely wide enough for you to stand. Its sides are made of smooth, slippery glass with no handhold or foothold. Water is up to your chin, and it's rising.

Then a voice comes down to you from above the pit. God is calling, "I'm throwing down a rope. If you'll just trust it enough to grab and hang on, I'll pull you up!" Sure enough, there's the rope—right in front of you—just within your reach.

Jesus is the rope. There isn't any other. He said so Himself.

What does it mean to grab and hang on? It means to have faith in Jesus Christ as the One who paid the price of your sins and who saves you. Faith is more than just head-belief. It means you stop trusting all the things you've trusted before and put your trust in Christ Jesus instead. It means you admit that you're a traitor and sinner and that you can't get back to God on your own. It means you say to the Lord with all your heart, mind, soul, and strength, "Jesus, I'm sorry. Please forgive me. Make me right inside. Mess with me. Do whatever you have to. Don't stop until I'm the way you want. Help me to follow and obey You. *I trust You, starting now!*"

You can't even *mean* such a prayer unless the Holy Spirit helps you, but He can. That's part of what He does. Start with the help He's giving you already. Whatever it is, accept it and ask His help for the next step. If you aren't really sorry for your sins, at least be sorry that you're not—and ask and trust Him to make you sorry for the rest. If you don't really trust Him for your salvation, at least start wanting to trust Him—and ask and trust Him to enable you to trust Him more. If you don't want to let go of your old life, at least desire that you could do so—and ask and trust Him to pry your fingers loose.

Through your life, as God pulls you up by the rope of Jesus, you'll pass through regions of glory as well as regions of discouragement. Remember as you pass through the regions of discouragement that you're being hauled through them by God whether you *feel* His presence or not. Tighten your grip! Remember as you pass through the regions of glory that the haul isn't finished even if you *feel* that it is. Tighten your grip again!

One day, when the long haul is over, the Lord Himself will welcome you to the top.

Chapter 3

WHAT THE WORLD THINKS OF ITSELF

MARS HILL

Ever since Adam and Eve first sinned, people have cooked up false gods and ungodly ideas about how things really are. They've done this to justify their rejection of the true God and what He says about how things really are. That may seem a strong statement, but the Bible doesn't agree with the view that it's hard to find out about God. It claims that people make it hard. The apostle Paul wrote that the truth about God was "plain" to the pagans and that in some sense they "knew" it, but that they "suppressed" it by their wickedness (Romans 1:18-23). Jesus made this even clearer by saying that those who seek will find. If this is true, then those who don't find aren't wholeheartedly seeking—they are just telling themselves that they are (Matthew 7:7-8).

In the ancient world, one of the places where all of the different gods and ideas were debated was the Greek city of Athens. Athens was filled with altars to pagan gods like Athena, Zeus, and Ares as well as teachers of pagan philosophies like Platonism, Stoicism, and Epicureanism. Even in the marketplace, the Athenians loved to hear of new teachings. They had a place called the Areopagus ("Mars Hill") where they spent all of their time hearing and telling about the philosophies, religions, and gods of their own land and others.

People all over the world considered the Athenians the wisest of the Greeks, but the Athenians themselves seemed to have mixed thoughts about the matter. On one hand, they sensed that their supposed wisdom was incomplete—

Notice the Date?

Seventy-five years ago, Western civilization despite inconsistencies was still predominantly Christian; today it is predominantly pagan.

—J. Gresham Machen,
Christianity and Liberalism
(1923)[1]

that something crucial was missing from it. An altar in the midst of the city was inscribed "To an Unknown God." One of their most famous philosophers, Socrates, used to say that the only thing he knew for sure was that he didn't know anything else for sure.

On the other hand, the Athenians covered up their doubts with pride. Although they liked listening to their "new things," they didn't really think anyone could teach them anything they didn't already know. As a result, the debates on Mars Hill were partly a search for truth, but partly just an intellectual game. The game might be called "Hide and Seek" because the players used various philosophies and religions as much to hide from God as to find Him.

We catch a glimpse of this intellectual game in the story of Paul's visit to Athens, told in the New Testament book of Acts. As soon as certain philosophers heard Paul teaching about Jesus in the market-place, they thought, "Something new!" and rushed him to Mars Hill to repeat his words there. But once they had him on Mars Hill, their attitude changed. Perhaps they expected Paul to teach a new *theory* about God. Instead he taught what God had *actually done.* The Resurrection was just too much for them; it was a little more reality than they wanted to deal with. Some of the listeners mocked Paul openly. Others—were they interested, or were they yawning?—told him to come back another time. So the Mars Hill lecture didn't exactly turn into a Billy Graham crusade. Yet a few listeners became believers— for instance, the Bible mentions a woman named Damaris and a man named Dionysius. Later there were more. In fact, historical documents suggest that Dionysius became the first bishop of the church in Athens.

Graffiti on a Campus Door
Written on the door is this: "How could a good God allow such doubt to enter my heart?" Every visit I make there, I pray that [the writer's] belief [may] be renewed.
—Anonymous college student

In the modern world, North America is much like Athens, and college is much like Mars Hill. Just as on Mars Hill, there are important things to learn at college. But there are also many false gods and ungodly philosophies. Just as on Mars Hill, students and teachers sense that there's something missing in all their learning. But they still think themselves wiser than anyone else. Just as on Mars Hill, the campus debates are only partly a search for truth and partly an intellectual game. But just as on Mars Hill, some people will listen and believe.

Today on campus, the most influential anti-Christian philosophies and outlooks include an old one called "Naturalism," a new one called "Postmodernism," and a religious attitude I call "Do-It-Yourself Spirituality." Let's give each of these a closer look.

NATURALISM

Naturalism is the belief that the material world of nature is all there is, all there ever has been, and all there ever will be—that nothing supernatural is real. If naturalism is true, then there isn't any God. For that matter, if naturalism is true there isn't anything at all except particles of matter in motion. Nothing else is real.

Most naturalists also think that the truth of naturalism is obvious to any rational person. Many even think it has somehow been proven by science. They conclude that faith is irrational, that belief in God is superstition, and that Christians are just too weak-minded to face the facts.

Most of your college teachers will probably be naturalists. How will you be able to tell? One student wrote to me about her experience in an ethics class. The textbook mentioned two main kinds of theories about where morality comes from: supernaturalistic and naturalistic. Supernaturalistic theories say morality comes from God; naturalistic theories say it doesn't. Unfortunately, the textbook considered only naturalistic theories. "When I asked the professor why it took such a narrow view," she said, "I was told that we would not have time for such superstitious and outdated theories." As you see, at first her professor tried to ignore Christianity. Then, when her question made ignoring it impossible, he simply treated it with contempt.

Some naturalists are even more contemptuous. A professor at a well-known denominational college used to hold up a Bible on the first day of every class and ask his students, "How many of you believe this book is the Word of God?" Perhaps one or two sheepishly raised their hands. At this he asked, "Do you want to know what I think of this book? *This* is what I think of it," and he hurled the Bible out the window.

But most naturalists prefer a more subtle approach. Instead of openly insulting Christianity, they patronize it—paying it the kind of compliments one pays to children and idiots. Or they use as-we-now-know statements: "*As we now know,* there is no life after death." These are often introduced by it-was-once-thought statements: "*It was once thought* that moral laws were given to us by a God or gods, but *as we now know,* mankind gives moral laws to himself." Whenever a teacher makes an as-we-now-know statement, ask "Who do you mean by 'we,' and how do we 'know'?" If you aren't yet ready for public debate, ask the questions inwardly. If you do ask them aloud, be respectful. Your goal isn't to show that your teacher is wrong, but merely that he isn't taking seriously the legitimate arguments on the other side.

The most aggressive naturalists are usually found in Darwinian biology departments, where belief in a Creator is either ignored or defined as unscientific. Don't be distracted: Our disagreement with naturalists isn't about whether God took millions of years to make us or only a short time; you can believe either way about that and still be a Christian. Our disagreement with naturalists is about whether God had anything to do with our appearance on the scene at all—whether we're "intended" or "accidental." "*As we now know,*" say naturalistic biologists, "man is the result of a purposeless and natural process that did not have us in mind."[3] Unfortunately, in this case it isn't enough to ask the teacher, "Who do you mean by 'we' and how do we 'know'?" He's got his answer ready for you. "We," he'll say, is "everyone familiar with the findings of science," and "how we know," he'll say, is that "scientific evidence overwhelmingly proves that Darwin was right." But you have an answer too, if you're willing to use it: More and more scientists, including naturalists, admit that the evidence doesn't prove any such thing![4]

Atheism As a Crutch

I want atheism to be true and am made uneasy by the fact that some of the most intelligent and well-informed people I know are religious believers. It isn't just that I don't believe in God and, naturally, hope that I'm right in my belief. It's that I hope there is not God! I don't want there to be a God; I don't want the universe to be like that. . . . My guess is that this cosmic authority problem is not a rare condition and that it is responsible for much of the scientism and reductionism of our time.

—Thomas Nagel, *The Last Word*[2]

To get this point across, ask your teacher to read the following words of Harvard paleontologist Richard Lewontin.[5] Like every naturalist, Lewontin believes that the material world of nature is all there is, but he also confesses to something many of his fellow naturalists would rather deny. The confession is that they all believe in naturalism *in spite* of the evidence, not because of it. For instance, even though the evidence strongly suggests that living things are the result of intelligent design, naturalists are desperate to prove they can't be.[6] Most of us would call the urge to ignore evidence "prejudice." Strangely, Lewontin calls it "taking the side of science"! See for yourself:

We take the side of science *in spite of* the patent absurdity of some of its constructs, . . . *in spite of* the tolerance of the scientific community for unsubstantiated just-so stories, because we have a prior commitment, a commitment to materialism. It is not that the methods and institutions of science somehow compel us to accept a material explanation of the phenomenal world, but, on the contrary, that we are forced by our *a priori* adherence to material causes to create an apparatus of investigation and a set of concepts that produce material explanations, no matter how counterintuitive, no matter how mystifying to the uninitiated. Moreover, that materialism is absolute, for we cannot allow a Divine Foot in the door.[7]

This amazing confession is important because it shows that what naturalists call "science" isn't really science—at least not if science means following the evidence! Naturalists like to think of themselves as brave defenders of clear reasoning against irrational superstition, but actually naturalism itself is the superstition. It isn't supported by reasoning, but by blind hostility to the evidence of God.

Postmodernism

Postmodernism is the belief that nothing hangs together—that everything is in pieces. For example:

A postmodernist thinks *truth* is fragmented. He doesn't believe in a truth that's the same for everyone, only in "stories" or "narratives" or "discourses" that are different for every group. One race tells a story about pioneers carving out civilization from the wilderness; another tells one about another race taking over their land. One religion tells one about God saving man; another tells one about man saving himself. If you try to ask, "But shouldn't we find out whether any of these stories is *true?*" the postmodernist will mutter something about "people who want to impose their stories on others."

A postmodernist thinks *personality* is fragmented. He doesn't believe in a soul, a self, an "I" that keeps its identity and is responsible for everything it does. At most, people wear masks or play roles— different at every moment. Sunday you play the role of Saint, Monday the role of Sinner. Tuesday you wear the mask of Nice Girl, Wednesday the mask of Tramp. If you try to ask, "But if I do play all these roles, isn't there a 'Me' that plays them? Under all my masks, isn't there a face?" the postmodernist will roll his eyes and say that you don't get it.

A postmodernist thinks *life* is fragmented. He doesn't believe his life is going anywhere, that it has a theme, that it's *about* anything—and he doesn't think yours is either. At most, he thinks, life is just a series of "projects" and relationships. January you're "with" one person, February you're "with" another. March you're "into" one activity, April you're "into" another. If you try to ask, "But shouldn't there be some kind of commitment or continuity to life—shouldn't it have a core?" the postmodernist will probably change the subject.

The biggest problem postmodernists face is meaninglessness. Different kinds of postmodernists cope with meaninglessness in different ways.

Macho postmodernists say, "Maybe

When We Finally Get Tired of Our Games
It is good to be tired and wearied by the vain search after the true good, that we may stretch out our arms to the Redeemer.
—Blaise Pascal, *Pensées*, no. 422 (1660)[8]

there isn't any meaning, but I'm brave enough to live without it." That's just a pose. They can't really live without meaning—they seek it in the idea of living bravely. The problem is that they don't have anything to be brave about.

Pop postmodernists say, "Meaning is a drag—who needs it? I'm so cool that I like life pointless." That's a pose too. They don't really like life pointless—they seek meaning in *seeming* to like it pointless, in being cool. The problem is that in a pointless life, being cool is as pointless as everything else is.

Political postmodernists say, "If I need a meaning, I'll get one from my group. Whatever we say is true, that's true for us." The problem is that there is no such thing as "true for us." If the group said rape were okay, would it be okay? If the group said babies were vermin, would they be vermin? If the group said a man and his dog were married, would they be married? In the eyes of the group, sure—but in reality, no. We can't change reality by changing the way we talk; we can only pretend to.

Most real-life postmodernists are a mix of the three flavors: a little macho, a dash of pop, and a sprinkling of political. Some of them wear the postmodernist label proudly. Others downplay their postmodernism—they say only "extreme" postmodernists believe there's no meaning, and they're not extremists. But meaninglessness is the *point* of postmodernism; there isn't much you can do to moderate it.

The "Foolishness" of the Cross

Has not God made foolish the wisdom of the world? For since in the wisdom of God the world through its wisdom did not know him, God was pleased through the foolishness of what was preached to save those who believe.

—1 Corinthians 1:20-21. You can read the entire passage in 1 Corinthians 1:17–2:10.

DO-IT-YOURSELF SPIRITUALITY

Do-it-yourself spirituality is the belief that everyone makes up his own view about God and ultimate reality, and that the best way to do this is to gather attractive ideas from various sources—from religions, from philosophies, even from movies and TV shows. I almost called this section "Spiritual Stew" because the do-it-yourselfer acts like an amateur cook, tossing all his chosen ingredients together and hoping the result won't taste too bad. One do-it-yourselfer may believe in reincarnation, crystals, and astrology. Another may believe in angels, saints, and channeling. Still another may have seen too many *Star Wars* movies and believe "the Force" is with him. Some do-it-yourselfers are hostile to organized religion, some belong to organized religions but pick and choose what to believe, and some even start their own religions (that's how Mormonism, Christian Science, and Scientology got started).

Because of this variety, I can't say "all do-it-yourselfers believe this" or "all do-it-yourselfers believe that." But I can tell you a few things they *usually* believe, and I can also tell you a few things they never— or at least never *consistently*—believe. First, the "usuallys":

Do-it-yourselfers usually believe that although the religions of the world differ greatly in rituals and formalities, they all really teach the same thing. Unfortunately, this is the opposite of the truth. As the writer G. K. Chesterton remarked, "The religions of the earth do not differ greatly in rites and forms; they do greatly differ in what they teach."[10] As though to prove the point, the people who claim that all religions teach the same thing all have different views of what that "same thing" is!

Do-it-yourselfers usually choose beliefs according to "what makes me feel good" rather than "what seems likely to be true." For instance, they may believe in reincarnation because it gives them many chances, in an easy-going God because He wouldn't take sins seriously, or in the godhood of every human being because they want to have things their own way.

Do-it-yourselfers usually put little stock in logical reasoning. Although there are exceptions, most do-it-yourselfers find logical reasoning a threat because it uncovers the flaws and inconsistencies in their worldviews. To brush off logical challenges, they say things like these: "Stop being so intolerant." "Reality is greater than logic." "Opposite beliefs can both be true at once." "This isn't about reasoning, it's about faith." "Nothing can be proven anyway, so what's the use?"

For Further Reading on Worldviews
James W. Sire, *The Universe Next Door: A Basic World View Catalog*, 3rd Edition.[9]

Now the "nevers."

Do-it-yourselfers never consistently believe that the Bible is a true revelation from God. The Bible condemns do-it-yourselfism. If do-it-yourselfers did believe it were a true revelation, how could they *consistently* go on being do-it-yourselfers? How could they *consistently* justify making up their own views about God and ultimate reality, if the truth about them was already written down?

Do-it-yourselfers never consistently believe what the Bible actually teaches. If do-it-yourselfers *consistently* believed what the Bible teaches, then they'd have to believe its condemnation of do-it-yourselfism. Some say they believe what it says, but they take its words out of context and twist the meanings. Often they justify their strange interpretations by claiming to have special insight that no one else possesses. For example, the founder of the Christian Science sect, Mary Baker Eddy, claimed to have the "key" to the Scriptures, and the founder of the Mormon sect, Joseph Smith, claimed to be the only person living with a "correct translation."

Do-it-yourselfers never consistently believe that Jesus was really who He said He was. If they *consistently* believed that He was who He said He was, then they would have to believe that He is the Way, the Truth, and the Life—and that would make do-it-yourselfism impossible (and unnecessary). Some say they believe that Jesus was who He said He was, but instead of seeking His meaning, they stuff His words with meanings of their own. For example, many people influenced by the new age movement say, "Yes, Jesus was God. We are all God." Needless to say, Jesus never taught that everyone is God!

GRAINS OF TRUTH

Let's take a look at the road we've traveled in this chapter. Like Mars Hill, college is full of different beliefs about God and ultimate reality. Although the debate about these worldviews goes on continually, it's only partly a search for truth. The other part is an intellectual game where the players pretend to be searching for truth but are really more interested in hiding from it. Many of your teachers will be *naturalists*—people who think the material world of nature is all there is. Some will be *methodological naturalists*—people who don't really believe that material nature is all there is, but confusedly think they should act as though it were. Quite a few will be *postmodernists*—people who think that life, truth, and personality are all fragmented, that nothing hangs together at all. You'll also meet many *spiritual do-it-yourselfers*—people who mix and match attractive ideas from all sorts of sources in order to whip up their own views about God and ultimate reality. Neither naturalism, postmodernism, nor do-it-yourselfism is compatible with biblical teaching.

Of course, naturalism contains a grain of truth, because nature is real. But naturalism goes wrong because material nature is not all there is. Greater than nature is God, who created it. Not only that, but He put much more into His creation than matter. He also put things into it like meaning, your soul, and right and wrong. That's why Christians aren't naturalists.

Postmodernism also contains a grain of truth, because when we try to live apart from God everything does fall apart. But postmodernism goes wrong because we don't have to live apart from God. He invites us back into fellowship with Him through Jesus Christ. When we accept His invitation, everything bent is made straight, and everything broken is made whole. That's why Christians aren't postmodernists.

Even do-it-yourself spirituality contains a grain of truth, because when we ignore God's own revelation it seems as though anything might be true. But do-it-yourselfers go wrong because we don't have to ignore God's revelation. It isn't necessary to whip up our own views of God and ultimate reality, because God Himself has told us the truth about the things we need to know. And that's why Christians aren't do-it-yourselfers.

Before ending this chapter I need to make a little confession. For the sake of clarity, I've given the three main campus worldviews names and explained them one at a time. By doing that, I may have given you two false impressions. One is that people *know what they are*—that naturalists know they're naturalists, postmodernists know they're postmodernists, and do-it-yourselfers know they're do-it-yourselfers. That's not how it is, because even at college quite a few people are unaware of what they really believe.

The other false impression is that naturalists, postmodernists, and do-it-yourselfers are *completely distinct groups,* like dogs, cats, and hamsters. That's not how it is either, because most people at college have been influenced by all three worldviews. For example some people are half-naturalist, half-postmodernist; they think "If nothing is real but material nature, then nothing has any meaning." Others are half-postmodernist, half-do-it-yourselfer; they think "If nothing has any meaning in itself, I can make up any meanings I want to."

The only firm rock in all this shifting sand is Jesus Christ. Hold on to Him, hold on to His Word, hold on to your partners in faith, and you'll be okay.

The Nine Top Errors of New Age Religion[11]

1. **Everything is one.**
   Contradicted in: **Genesis 1**
2. **Everything is God.**
   Contradicted in: **Romans 1:18-25**
3. **I myself am God.**
   Contradicted in: **Ezekiel 28:1-9**
4. **I can save myself.**
   Contradicted in: **Ephesians 2:8-9**
5. **After I die I will be reincarnated.**
   Contradicted in: **Hebrews 9:27**
6. **All morality is relative.**
   Contradicted in: **Exodus 20:1-17; Matthew 5:17-20**
7. **All "spirits" and everything "spiritual" is good.**
   Contradicted in: **Deuteronomy 18:9-14**
8. **Humans are evolving toward a harmonious New Age.**
   Contradicted in: **1 Thessalonians 5:3; Matthew 24:3-31**
9. **All religions really teach the same thing.**
   Contradicted in: **John 14:6; Acts 4:12**

Chapter 4

Talking with NonChristian Friends

When Julie got to college she was put in a dorm room with three other women. They talked about everything; it seemed they never stopped. Ruth said she was a "very spiritual person" but didn't believe in organized religion. Sally was a New Ager who burned incense and talked a lot about her "Higher Self." Amy had been to church a few times and "guessed she was a Christian," but believed in reincarnation and listened raptly to everything Sally said. When Julie said Jesus Christ was the most important thing in her life, the others were all warmly supportive, so Julie thought their warmth was a response to the gospel message. But they turned out to be just as warmly supportive when Ruth said mountain biking was the most important thing in her life, Sally said her "inner godhood" was the most important thing in her life, and Amy said, "I think we're all really saying the same thing." Julie was baffled.

When Mike took a class in organic chemistry, he joined a study group organized by two of his classmates. Nobody kept order, and sometimes the discussion got off the track. Every now and then it turned to religion. There was a guy named Tom who seemed to get all his religious ideas from *Star Trek: The Next Generation* and talked about the characters as though they were real people. Then there were Stan, the evolutionist; Dan, the agnostic; and Fran, who wouldn't say what she believed. One day Mike mentioned that he was a Christian. The others just ignored him, so he never mentioned his faith again.

You'll have many friends and acquaintances at college, and they won't all be Christians. Naturally, you'll want to share your faith with them. But how? In some ways it's much easier now than it was in your parents' day. Back then people used to say "this is a Christian country," and as a result the identity of the Christian faith was blurred. People tended to assume that everyone was a Christian, or at least that everyone who worked hard and stayed out of trouble was a Christian. One result was that a person could live his whole life without knowing that he wasn't a Christian, so you didn't know who to evangelize. Another was that Christianity seemed part of the "Establishment," so if people were angry about anything, they were angry with Christianity too. All that has changed. Now, very few people say "this is a Christian country." People who aren't Christians usually know they aren't Christians, so you know who to evangelize. Being a Christian no longer seems like the "Establishment" thing to do; in fact, it even seems daring and countercultural. So in all these ways sharing your faith has become easier.

But in other ways, sharing your faith has become harder. In your parents' day, even people who had never set foot in a church knew *something* about the Christian faith. They knew the Bible has an Old and a New Testament. They knew it says there is only one God. They knew who Abraham and Moses were. They knew what the Ten Commandments were. They knew about heaven and hell. They knew Jesus was supposed to be God in human form. They knew that He was supposed to have been born among us as a baby and lived among us as a man. They knew He was supposed to have died on a cross for our sins and risen to life after three days. All that has changed too. You can't take it for granted that people know anything about Christianity anymore. Even people who have gone to church all their lives (or say they have) may be completely ignorant about what Christians believe. Not only that, today Christianity is often treated with hostility.

This is a thoroughly practical chapter, written to help you speak with your college friends and acquaintances about Jesus Christ. First comes a short section with advice about getting started. Next comes a long section about how to deal with your friends' questions. The reason it's so long is that questions come in three different varieties, each of which needs to be handled differently: plain questions, questions that pose objections, and questions that are really smokescreens for other issues that remain hidden. We'll also talk about how to deal with lifestyle conflicts—friction that results from the contrast between how you live and how some of your nonbelieving friends might live. Finally we'll talk about who influences whom—that difficult problem of how to spend time with nonbelievers without letting their worldviews and lifestyles rub off on you.

GETTING STARTED

The best advice I can give about getting started is (1) pray, (2) pray, (3) pray, (4) pray, (5) pray, (6) pray, and (7) pray. That's seven "prays." Let me explain what I mean.

First, pray for the *chance* to share your faith. A few years after my own conversion, Christ strengthened in me the desire to tell others about Him. But how could I do it? The opportunity never seemed to arise. I prayed, "Lord, You've promised that Your power is made perfect in our weakness. I don't even know how to begin a conversation about You. Please give me openings. And please, Lord, make them so obvious that even I can't fail to see them." That week, on three separate occasions, three different people asked *me* about God. Each time the question was completely unexpected, as though it had dropped from a clear blue sky. I knew God was answering my prayer.

Second, pray to *be ready* to share your faith. If you pray for opportunities God will send them, but if you're not ready you may not even notice them. Case: You and your racquetball partner are showering down after a game. He mentions some personal problems and says, "I wonder if God even knows I'm alive." Case: You and your roommate are standing in the supermarket checkout line next to the magazine rack. He catches your eye, grins, and points to a tabloid with the headline "Scientists Report: Jesus a Space Alien." Case: You're sharing some burgers with a classmate from mainland China. She says, "Once in my country we were all supposed to believe in Communism. Now young people like me wonder what to believe."

Third, pray for *discretion* in sharing your faith. Just as there is a time and place to talk, there is a time and place *not* to talk. In the story of Julie and her roommates in the first section of this chapter, Julie might have gained more ground looking for an opportunity to speak to each friend in private rather than when they were all together. Being in one room seemed to put the girls in "warm fuzzy mode"—they wanted to "support" each other and were in no state of mind to consider whether any of the things that were being said were actually good or true. In the story of Mike and his study group, Mike was probably right to shut up when he did. You can't make people listen when they don't want to, and if you try, you may be asking for trouble (Matthew 7:6). However, rather than being discouraged he should have stayed alert for another opportunity. Someone might have been interested in what he said but been afraid to let on. God might have opened a door for Mike to speak on a later occasion.

Practical Evangelism

One of the best resources for learning how to share the gospel with your nonChristian friends is the "Effective Evangelism" column in *Christian Research Journal*. Each month a different writer offers practical suggestions for dealing with a particular problem or issue. Previous columns can be accessed through the ICL search engine at http://www.iclnet.org/search.html. Type *Effective Evangelism Christian Research Journal* and click on "Search."

Fourth, pray for *words* to share your faith. There's a sense in which you can prepare, and another sense in which you can't. You can prepare by walking with God, studying and memorizing Scripture, trading evangelism stories with Christian friends, and reading books like this. But you can't prepare in the sense that you can't know ahead of time exactly what issues might come up in a conversation, what factors might lie behind them, and what your friend may need most to hear. Pray not only before you speak, but as you are speaking. "For it will not be you speaking, but the Spirit of your Father speaking through you" (Matthew 10:20). And remember what has to go along with your words. There's a saying among Christians: "Don't talk the talk unless you walk the walk." This means that if you merely talk like a Christian and don't live like a Christian, Christ can't use you. Your life has to be like His. That should be included in your prayer.

Fifth, pray for patience to *listen* as you share your faith. Have you ever punched the print button to make a single photocopy, only to find that the machine was set to make a hundred copies and you didn't know how to make it stop? You don't want your friend to feel as though you're that machine. If you can't hear him, he won't be able to hear you. It isn't your job to "print out" everything you know.

Sixth, pray for God to *prepare your friend's heart and mind* as you share your faith. You can't reconcile someone with God; only God can do that. Only He can break down the inner barriers. We human beings need God's help even to *want* His help, much less to accept it.

Seventh, pray to *thank* God for the opportunity to glorify His name. Don't worry whether your friend received Christ or not; pray anyway. You may never know how God has used you. To explain this, the apostle Paul used the language of farming. One person may plant the seeds, another may water the seeds that someone else plants, and still another may harvest the crop. In the same way, God may use one person merely to get someone thinking, another to explain the gospel to him, and another to lead him to faith in Christ. "So neither he who plants nor he who waters is anything, but only God, who makes things grow" (1 Corinthians 3:7).

Great Classics for Seekers

For your practical friends:
    John R. W. Stott, *Basic Christianity*, 2nd edition.[1]

For your intellectual friends:
    C. S. Lewis, *Mere Christianity*.[2]

A final thought. The title of this section is "Getting Started." That doesn't just mean starting to share your faith. If a friend receives Christ, then it means starting out in a relationship with a new brother or sister in Christ! Introduce your friend to other Christians. Take him to your college Christian fellowship. Take him to church. Do things together, show him the ropes, model the life of Christ. He's part of the family now.

How to Deal with Questions

Plain Questions

A "plain question" is a simple request for information. If a friend raises a plain question, he isn't objecting to Christianity—he's just trying to find out something about it. You don't need to be a genius to figure out what to do with a plain question. Just answer it! Here are some examples of plain questions, along with the answers I might give.

Question: Is "Christ" a last name, like "Jones"?

Answer: No, it's another word for Messiah. It's a title. "Jesus Christ" means "Jesus, the Chosen One of God."

Question: Chosen for what?

Answer: Chosen to be the Path back to the Father—to be what we call "Savior."

Question: What does that mean, "Savior"?

Answer: "Savior" means "Rescuer." We need to be rescued from our sin and separation from God, because we can't fix these problems just by trying.

Question: Somebody told me Jesus is "Savior and Lord." Does "Lord" mean "God"?

Answer: It's true that Jesus is God, but the title "Lord" just means "Boss."

Question: I keep hearing Christians talk about the "gospel." What's that?

Answer: "Gospel" means "good news." The gospel is the good news that even though we human beings have rebelled against God and messed ourselves up, He came and offered us a way back to Him through faith in Jesus Christ.

Question: Is that where all that stuff about Jesus "dying for our sins" comes in?

Answer: Yes, because the punishment for sin is death, and He took our punishment on our behalf. It's like if you were desperate because you didn't have any money to pay your debt, but I had money and paid it for you.

Question: He would do that for me?

Answer: Yes, because He loves you. He'd do it for anybody who is truly sorry for his sins and ready to trust Him as Rescuer and Boss forever.

Question: So why did you become a Christian?

Answer: I'm a Christian because at one point in my life I realized that I was separated from God and could only get back to Him through Jesus Christ.

Question: When you became a Christian, did you feel any different?

Answer: Well, I did, but not everybody does. The important thing isn't how you feel
but the reality of what God is actually doing.

Question: So what would happen if I became a Christian?

Answer: The immediate change is that all your sins would be forgiven and you'd be
accepted into God's family forever—kind of like being adopted. The grad-
ual change is that God would change you from within. That part takes a lot
of work from you, but the real power to change comes from Him.

Keep your answers short and simple, and avoid "churchy" words. Try to phrase your answers in a
way that sparks further interest. If you don't have the answer to your friend's question, admit that you
don't and promise to get help to find it. Just remember to keep your promise!

Objections

An objection expresses a person's deeper qualms about the Christian faith—perhaps uneasiness about
puzzling ideas. These can often become a reason your friend gives *not* to trust Jesus as Lord and Savior.
Because objections can take the form of questions, sometimes plain questions and objections are hard to
tell apart. What difference does it make? If your friend asks you a plain question you simply need to give
him information, but if he presents an objection you need to try to solve his puzzle.

Let me illustrate. Matthew had shared his faith with two friends, Mary and Carmen. They were twin sisters and lived together. One day while he was walking to class with Mary, she said, "Carmen and I were talking about what you'd told us, and we have a question. Why did Jesus have to pray?"

Matthew wasn't sure what Mary was getting at, so he replied with a question of his own: "What is it
about His praying that puzzles you?"

She answered, "Well, I guess I'm just confused about prayer in general. Why did He do it? Why does
anybody do it?"

Because she seemed to be making a simple request for information, Matthew provided it. "Jesus
needed to pray for the same reason all people need to pray, Mary—to stay in touch with God."

Later that day, Matthew bumped into Carmen. "Oh, hi," she said. "Did Mary ask you our question?"

"Do you mean why Jesus had to pray?" he asked.

"Yes," she said. "What's the answer?"

Assuming that the same thing was on both sisters' minds, Matthew began to tell Carmen the same thing he had told Mary. To his surprise, she interrupted before he could finish.

"No," she said, "you don't get it. I know what prayer is for. What's puzzling me is that if Jesus prayed, then you must have been wrong when you said Jesus was God. He couldn't pray to Himself!" Only then did Matthew realize that Carmen wasn't just asking for information, as Mary had—she was presenting a puzzle and demanding the solution!

So he changed course and provided it. "God has three Persons, Carmen—you could say He's one *What* but three *Whos.* When Jesus prayed, that was God the Son talking with God the Father." Carmen seemed satisfied.

Do you see? The two sisters had said the same *words*—"Why did Jesus have to pray?"—but they were getting at different things. Mary was posing a plain question, but Carmen was posing an objection. Each friend had to be answered differently.

Sometimes it's crystal clear that your friend is posing *some* objection, but the problem is to figure out *what* objection! This requires what the Bible calls "discernment." Let me tell you another story.

Priscilla had also told two friends about Christ. One was named Mark, the other Tom. She and Mark shared a European history class. One day after hearing a lecture about the millions of deaths in World War I, Mark asked her, "If God is as good and powerful as you say He is, then how can He permit suffering?"

Priscilla realized immediately that Mark was stating an objection, and here's the answer she gave him: "Mark, I think you're trying to say that a good and powerful God *couldn't* permit suffering. But what if the only way to stop us from hurting each other was to take away our free will? God wouldn't do that—He wants sons and daughters, not robots."

Mark was silent for a moment, then said, "That helps. I'll think about it."

Don't *Be* Apologetic—*Do* Apologetics!

Apologetics (from the Greek word *apologion*) is the defense of the Christian faith against objections. If you really want to be able to answer your friends, read the *Handbook of Christian Apologetics* by Peter Kreeft and Ronald K. Tacelli.[3] Also good (though more specialized) is *When Skeptics Ask: A Handbook of Christian Evidence* by Ron Brooks and Norman L. Geisler.[4] If you'd rather browse, many good apologetics resources can be found on the Leadership U website: http://www.leaderu.com/, and the Probe Ministries Theology/Apologetics webpage: http://www.probe.org/menus/wp-theol.html.

Later the same day, Priscilla met her other friend, Tom, for a hamburger. The subject turned to religion, and guess what? Tom posed the same objection Mark had posed. Or at least it seemed to be the same. "Priscilla, you say God is all-good and all-powerful. If that's true, then how can He permit suffering?"

What a coincidence! thought Priscilla, and she launched right into her little speech about free will. Tom heard her out, but by the time she finished, he seemed angry.

"Look, Priscilla," he said. "My father ran off with his secretary, my mother's got cancer, and we haven't heard from my drug-addict brother in years. I ask you why your God permits suffering, and you give me a philosophy lecture? That stuff might get you an A on some term paper, but in real life it just doesn't cut it."

Stunned, Priscilla was silent for a long time. Then she looked him full in the face and said, "I'm sorry, Tom. I didn't know about those things." She paused. "Maybe what you're really asking is how you can trust a God who let them happen." Tom just looked at her; he wasn't going to make this easy. She went on anyway. "Look, I don't have all the answers. I don't know everything about why God permits suffering, but I know how He feels about it. He came down and took the worst of it upon Himself. He *died* for you, Tom."

Tom stared at her for a full thirty seconds. She couldn't read his face at all. "Well, maybe," he grunted. "I'll think about it."

Do you see? On the surface, Mark and Tom were expressing the same objection to Christianity, but their underlying concerns were completely different. Mark's was intellectual, and he needed an intellectual answer. Tom's was personal, and he needed a personal answer. So be sure you understand what your friend is *really* asking before you answer. Look before you leap.

Smokescreens

The hardest habit to break in talking with nonChristian friends is thinking that we have to take every question and objection seriously. But don't we? In one sense, yes: You should never treat a friend with disrespect. But in another sense, no: Some questions and objections aren't *intended* seriously. They're not real questions or objections. They're not ways of getting at the truth, but ways of hiding from it. They're smokescreens.

When someone poses a real question, you answer it. If someone raises a real objection, you try to solve the puzzle. But if someone stirs up a cloud of smoke, you should blow it away—if you can. Let me show you what I mean.

One way to disperse a smokescreen is to toss the question right back at the questioner. "Morals are all relative anyway," said Tom. "How do we even know that murder is wrong?" The question was a smokescreen, and his friend Frank knew it was. Every human alive knows that murder is wrong; some just pretend they don't.

So Frank asked, "Are you in *real doubt* that murder is wrong?"

Tom's first response was evasive: "Many people might say it's all right."

"But I'm not asking other people," pressed Frank. "Are you at this moment in any real doubt about murder being wrong for everyone?"

There was a long silence. "No," Tom admitted. "No, I'm not."

"Good," Frank answered. "Then we don't have to waste time on morals being relative. Let's talk about something you *really are* in doubt about." A few moments passed as Tom realized that his smokescreen, his "cover," had been blown away—then he agreed.

Another way to disperse a smokescreen is what I call "play-back."

"You've asked a lot of questions," I said to one young friend. "Have you noticed a pattern in our conversation?"

"What do you mean?" he asked.

"I mean," I returned, "that you interrupt each of my answers by asking another question from a different direction."

He thought about that. "I guess I do," he said. "Why do I do that?"

"Why do you think?" I countered.

"I guess because I don't want to hear your answers," he replied.

"Okay, then," I said to him, "let's

God Has Gone Before You

The Bible mentions at least five ways in which God has *already* made a little bit about Himself and His moral requirements known to all human beings. So even before you share the gospel, God has prepared the way.

1. *The testimony of creation,* which speaks to all people of a glorious, powerful, and merciful Creator (Psalm 19:1-6; Psalm 104; Acts 14:17; Romans 1:20). *You can explain that He cares.*
2. *The hints placed in our longings,* which make us aware of an Unknown God who is different from all of our idols (Genesis 1:26-27; Acts 17:22-23). *You can explain who He is.*
3. *The principles embodied in our design,* our physical and emotional blueprint, where a variety of God's purposes are plain to see (Romans 1:26-27). *You can explain that He has spoken.*
4. *The principle of the harvest,* that what we sow we reap, which teaches us by linking every sin with consequences (Galatians 6:7). *You can explain that He heals.*
5. *The law of conscience,* written on the human heart, so that deep down we all know we have a sin problem (Romans 2:14-15). *You can explain the solution: Jesus Christ.*

talk about why you don't." Finally he stopped playing games, and our conversation began to get somewhere.

A third approach is to hold up a mirror. Mark had dozens of objections to Terry's Christian views. Whenever Terry shot one objection down, Mark just deployed another. Before long Terry realized that Mark was simply laying down a smoke barrage—that Mark may have thought he cared about Terry's answers, but he didn't really.

"Tell me something," Terry asked. "Suppose we took a few weeks and I answered every one of your objections to your complete intellectual satisfaction."

"Okay," said Mark. "I'm supposing."

"Good," said Terry. "*Then* would you become a Christian?"

Mark's face registered shock as he realized that his answer was no. All of those beautiful objections—why, they weren't his real reasons for rejecting Jesus Christ at all! He just *didn't want* Jesus. Though he was still far from receiving Christ as Lord and Savior, he'd turned a corner; he'd finally begun to be honest with himself.

Not every smokescreen can be dispersed. If your friend won't stop blowing smoke, leave him alone. Give him time. Maybe he'll come around someday, and maybe he won't; leave him to God. I'm not saying you can't be his friend; I'm saying you have to be realistic. For now, stop talking to him about Jesus. This isn't just my advice—it's God's command. Jesus said, "Do not give dogs what is sacred; do not throw your pearls to pigs. If you do, they may trample them under their feet, and then turn and tear you to pieces" (Matthew 7:6). That's shocking language—but smokescreens are a shocking problem.

HOW TO DEAL WITH LIFESTYLE CONFLICTS

So far in this chapter on talking with nonChristian friends we've been focusing on how they *think.* But it can also be tough to talk with them because of how they *live,* can't it? Lifestyle differences cause problems in at least four different ways.

Scarcity of activities you can share. All friends have something in common. The deepest friendships are based on shared faith in the risen Lord. Because you don't yet share faith with your nonChristian friends, your friendships will probably be based on activities you both enjoy. You may run with Earl, watch old movies with Margo, and tinker with computers with Luis. The problem is that just as shared activities can bring you together, activities you can't share divide you. Liz likes to get drunk, Stan spends a lot of time on drugs, and Renaldo "cruises," looking for women to have sex with him.

You can't share these activities because they grieve the Holy Spirit. So what do you do?

One thing you can do is invite your acquaintances along on *your* activities. Getting together a Superbowl party? Going to church? Got tickets to a concert or sporting match? Ask Liz, Stan, or Renaldo along. But you also need to accept the fact that your relationships with your nonChristian acquaintances may remain limited. Not everyone will be interested in your invitations. With some people you may never share anything more than the activity that first brought you together—even if it's just talking together during breaks at the place where you both work part-time. Do what you can with what you've got.

Demands you can't meet. From time to time your nonChristian friends may demand things from you that no Christian can give. The most common are demands that you do something you can't do, approve something you can't approve, or allow something you can't allow. For instance, Keesha may be angry because you won't sleep with her, Kay may call you a bigot because you won't say "gay is good," and Karl may give you a hard time because you won't let him bring dope to your party.

The four basic guidelines are Don't Argue, Don't Apologize, Don't Back Down, and Don't Get Trapped.

Don't argue means don't let yourself be drawn into a shouting match or debate.

Don't apologize means don't feel guilty or make excuses about refusing what you know is wrong.

Don't back down means stand your ground without wavering or changing your mind.

Don't get trapped means avoid situations where you may be tempted to give in.

The last guideline may need some explanation. What kinds of situations might tempt you to give in? Let's use Keesha as an example again. If you know she has the hots for you, then you shouldn't be kissing her in the first place. Don't tell yourself, "I'll stop before I've gone too far"; just don't start. In fact, you shouldn't be alone with her at all. Who do you think you are, the Man of Steel? Another way of getting trapped is to think you can "play counselor" when she's telling you her life story and sniffling tearfully about how nobody has ever liked her. In the first place you aren't trained as a counselor. In the second place she belongs to the other sex. What you call "compassion" might just be your hormones in disguise.

Your friend's other friends. Sometimes problems arise not from lifestyle conflicts with your friend, but from lifestyle conflicts with the people who hang around your friend. For example, maybe Karl doesn't do drugs, but his roommates are fried all the time. That problem is easy because you don't

Three Good Times to Strike Up a Conversation About Faith

1. In a foxhole (strong motivation)
2. On a long drive (no distractions)
3. Over a meal (easy to talk)

have to go to Karl's place anyway. Go to a movie with him, shoot some hoops, find some other place to spend time together.

A harder case is when the "friends of the friend" want to tag along. Still harder is when they try to cause divisions between you. Hardest of all is when they tag along *and* try to cause divisions. This makes your own friendship impossible, and you have to say so. If your friend is willing to talk about the problem, fine. If not, find another friend.

Physical and spiritual danger. Some people are just plain dangerous. Your obligation to bear witness to Christ doesn't mean you have to hang around with those who might physically or spiritually hurt you. Don't imagine that dangerous types don't exist on campus, don't imagine that you can make them less dangerous, and don't imagine that you're somehow immune from harm—just stay away from them. Among the kinds to avoid are people prone to violence, people involved in criminal activity, people into Satanic occultism, and people who might get you in trouble. If you already have relationships with them, break them off. Now. You don't have to explain; just bug out. It isn't that Christ doesn't want to reach them, but that you're not equipped for the job. Leave them to specially trained counselors and ministers.

WHO INFLUENCES WHOM

My last piece of advice is *Remember Whose You Are!* Please notice that I didn't say *who* you are; I said *whose* you are. You belong to Jesus Christ. God wants to use you to reach your nonChristian friends—but Satan wants to use your nonChristian friends to reach you. Don't let him turn the tables.

Satan will try to turn the tables by making you feel embarrassed about your faith—by making you think that it's childish, silly, or intolerant. Another way is to pull you away from your partners in faith—to make you feel that "your kind of people" aren't the ones who worship the same Lord, but the ones who pledge the same club or have the same color of skin. Still another way is to weaken your discipline and suck you into sin—especially into an entwining, addicting sin like drunkenness, drugs, or sex. That strategy is one of the Enemy's favorites because not many of us human beings doubt God and then start sinning. Most of us start sinning and then doubt God.

Satan can use your nonChristian friends in all of these ways to get to you. God wants you to rub off

> ## Three Bad Times to Strike Up a Conversation About Faith
> 1. At a rock concert (no motivation)
> 2. At a party (too many distractions)
> 3. At a movie (who wants to talk?)

on them, but the Enemy wants them to rub off on you. So remember: You can have friends outside the faith, but for your deepest comrades you should look to your brothers and sisters in Christ. Hang out with the holy. Get in with the godly. Spend time with the saved. Know who your real family is, the one where the Father is God.

"I Was in Prison and You Came to Visit Me."
—Matthew 25:36

Founded in 1976 by Chuck Colson, Prison Fellowship has helped many people that no one else has been able to. The organization organizes and trains volunteers for a variety of ministries to prisoners, ex-prisoners, their families, and the victims of crime. Phone (703) 478-0010 or visit the website at http://www.pfm.org/.

Campus Myths

Chapter 5

Myths About the Search for Knowledge

Hot Stuff

Truth is hot, scary stuff. Truth about God is the hottest of all. It scares some people so badly that they don't even want to search for it. One day in a "great books" course my students were discussing the great medieval thinker Thomas Aquinas. Thomas Aquinas had been a Christian, and some of the students were interested in what he believed about God. As they explored his views, one young man became more and more agitated. Finally he said, "This isn't helping me," and asked whether he could just pick up the assignment and leave. Of course, I said he could.

Later he visited my office, and I found out what his problem was. He told me that he wasn't interested in truth—that the only thing he cared about was what had immediate practical value for him. Searching for truth about God, it seemed, was especially impractical because if he found it, his whole world might turn upside down.

Or could it be that it would turn rightside up?

The Rundown

On campus you'll meet dozens of myths about the search for truth, but most of them are variations on ones that I'm going to discuss. For convenience I've divided them into *general myths* (the ones you might hear from almost anyone), *skeptical myths* (the ones you'll hear from people who despair of finding any truth at all), and *relativist myths* (the ones you'll hear from people who believe that we all have truth, but yours might be different from mine).

Labels like *skeptic* and *relativist* go in and out of fashion, and other labels take their place. For example someone might tell you that he's not a skeptic but a "postmodernist," or that he's not a relativist but a "multiculturalist." Don't worry about that. Listen to what people say, not to what they call themselves. Ask them to cut out the jargon and tell you in plain words what they think.

GENERAL MYTHS

Myth Number One: Thinking you know the truth is arrogant and intolerant.

Your history teacher has just finished lecturing on world religions. As you're packing up your books to leave, a classmate remarks, "I figure every road to God is as good as every other, don't you think?"

You reply, "No, I think the Bible's right when it says there's only one."

Annoyed, your classmate says, "So who made *you* God?"

All day long as you go about your business, you worry about whether he was right. *Is* it arrogant and intolerant to think you know the truth about something?

Why would anyone think it is? I happen to know that the potato salad is spoiled, and the last three diners got sick just from eating it. Would you call me arrogant to warn the others? I happen to know that the public library is this direction, but the motorist who asked me for directions is headed the other way. Would you call me intolerant to suggest that he turn around? Of course not. Then how is what you said different? It sounded pretty modest to me. You didn't even claim personal authority because you gave the credit for what you know to the Bible.

The people who call Christians intolerant have an answer to this. "We're talking about matters of *opinion*," they say. "Food spoilage and highway directions are matters of *fact*." Of course they're matters of fact. The potato salad really is spoiled, and the public library really is that direction. But that doesn't mean they aren't matters of opinion too! After all, people may have different opinions about just what the facts *are*.

Differences of opinion arise even in the sciences. Paleontologist Stephen Jay Gould is of the opinion that Darwinian evolution is a fact; biochemist Michael J. Behe is of the opinion that it's not. Each scientist says that he's right; each scientist says that the other is wrong. Does that make him arrogant or intolerant? No—not so long as he offers evidence for what he thinks, listens to the evidence offered by his opponent, and doesn't try to shut him up. That's how science is supposed to work.

What gives power to the myth that says "having truth is intolerant"? Its power comes from a picture—not a photograph or a painting, but an image many people carry in their minds. In this picture, a man is being burned at the stake. He's there because other people, who say they have the truth, are angry with him for saying that they don't.

Yes, that's a terrible picture. I agree that what it shows should never happen. But in my mind is a different picture. In mine a man is being burned at the stake too, but for a completely different reason. He's there because other people, who say there *isn't* any truth, are angry with him for saying that there *is*.

Do you see my point? Doubters can be just as intolerant as believers—and if you don't believe me now, you will after you've spent a little time at college! In fact, wasn't the imaginary classmate who called you intolerant a bit intolerant himself? Did he offer evidence for what *he* thinks? Did he listen to your evidence? Or did he merely try to shut you up?

The apostle Peter says, "Always be prepared to give an answer to everyone who asks you to give the reason for the hope you have. But do this with gentleness and respect, keeping a clear conscience, so that those who speak maliciously against your good behavior in Christ may be ashamed of their slander" (1 Peter 3:15-16). Arrogance doesn't come from having convictions about the truth; it comes from having the *wrong* convictions about how to treat people who don't share it with you. Humility doesn't come from not having any convictions; it comes from having the *right* convictions about the importance of gentleness and respect.

Myth Number Two: The important thing in life isn't having truth, but searching for it.

You're more likely to hear this particular myth from burned-out teachers than from other students. You may also meet it in books. For instance, one of the most famous of living philosophers suggested that the good life is a life spent seeking the good life. I mean no disrespect to him, for I've learned from some of his work myself. But do you notice something fishy here? He's talking in circles. On one hand, he says he already knows what the good life is—it's the life spent in seeking the good life. But if he already knows what the good life is, then he doesn't have to seek it. On the other hand, if he does still seek the good life, then he doesn't yet know what it is. And if he doesn't yet know what it is, he has no business telling us that he does!

Would you listen for even a moment if someone tried to tell you it was better to itch than to scratch, to be hungry than to eat, or to seek friends than to have them? No? Then why would anyone believe that it's better to seek truth than to find it? Why should this desire and search be different than any other?

Do you know what I think? I think God has given us two different kinds of desire for truth—one for truth with a little *t*, and another for truth with a capital *T*. Truth with a little *t* is abstract knowledge. The desire for this kind of truth is satisfied by knowing things like what makes a great poem beautiful, what stars really are, how plants and animals are made, and how many gods there are. This truth is good knowledge, some of it even crucial knowledge, but the kind you can write on a blackboard.

Now Truth with a capital *T* is something else altogether. It's God Himself in person. The desire for *this* Truth can be satisfied only by *personal* knowledge, *living* knowledge—the greatest knowledge, but the kind you can have only through relationship with Him.

Some teachers and scholars burn out because they confuse the two desires. They try to satisfy their longing for Truth with a capital *T* merely by piling up more and more truth with a little *t*. The problem is that although truth has its own satisfaction, it can't give you the satisfaction of Truth. Confusing the two desires is like trying to relieve an itch by eating a hamburger! If you keep on asking from *t*ruth what only *T*ruth can give, eventually it can't even give you what it gave before. The only sweetness left to you is the sweetness of the memory of the longing itself. So you tell yourself, "Now I understand. The important thing in life isn't having truth, but longing and searching for it."

And then you tell your students. And then you tell your friends. And then you write it in your books. But it's all wrong. Have compassion for your burned-out teachers, but don't repeat their mistake.

Myth Number Three: Faith hinders the search for truth because it gets in the way of reasoning.

This myth has been around for centuries, and it's deeply ingrained in the way college people think. Some students will begin to groan as soon as they learn you're a Christian. They'll try to give you history lessons. "I thought we'd escaped from the Dark Ages," they'll chide. "Wasn't there a little thing called the Enlightenment?"

Here's the main thing to understand. To say that faith gets in the way of reasoning stands facts on their head, for reasoning itself depends on faith. Did you hear that? Reasoning itself depends on faith. Can you see why? Imagine that someone says to you, "All reasoning is baloney." He's wrong, of course, but can you prove it? Guess what? You can't. The only way to show that reasoning isn't baloney would be to reason about it. But in that case your argument would be circular—and one of the rules of good reasoning is that circular arguments don't prove anything! So how *do* we know that reasoning isn't baloney? We take it on trust. And trust is another word for faith.

Reasoning depends on trust, on faith, in other ways too. How do you know the moon is made of rock instead of cheese? You say people have been there and found out. But did you go along to make sure? Of course not; you just trust that they were telling the truth. *Faith.*

If you're scientifically inclined, maybe you'll add that the moon doesn't reflect light in the same way as cheese. But have you compared the reflections from rock and cheese yourself? Of course not; you just trust that someone has. *Faith.*

What if I speculated that on the moon, cheese reflects light as rock does on earth and rock reflects light as cheese does on earth? Maybe you'll answer that the laws of physics don't change from place to place. But have you personally checked all the places in the universe to be sure? Of course not; you just trust that nature doesn't play tricks. *Faith.*

I'm not saying that all kinds of faith are true; I'm just saying that you can't do without it. The plain fact is that unless you have *some* faith, you can't reason even an inch. Unless you have *some* trust, you can't even decide what to doubt. You have to believe something in order to know anything. *Even atheists have faith.* They take it on trust that matter is all there is. I think that's an error—but it's faith.

The Reasonableness of Revelation

How . . . possible is it (if indeed there are degrees of possibility) to penetrate into the thoughts of Almighty God? His mind is infinite. His thoughts tower above our thoughts as the heavens tower above the earth. It is ludicrous to suppose that we could ever penetrate into the mind of God. There is no ladder by which our little minds can climb up into His infinite mind. There is no bridge that we can throw across the chasm of infinity. There is no way to reach or to fathom God.

It is only reasonable to say, therefore, that unless God takes the initiative to disclose what is in His mind, we shall never be able to find out. Unless God makes Himself known to us, we can never know Him, and all the world's altars—like the one Paul saw in Athens—will bear the tragic inscription, "To An Unknown God" (Acts 17:23).

This is the place to begin our study. It is the place of humility before the infinite God. It is also the place of wisdom, as we perceive the reasonableness of the idea of revelation.

—John R.W. Stott, *You Can Trust the Bible*[1]

So whether to have faith isn't an issue. You *will* have faith in something—if not in God, then something else. The only real question is which kind of faith to have. The wrong kind will hinder the search for truth—but the right kind will help.

SKEPTICAL MYTHS

Myth Number Four: There isn't any truth.

I'm not sure why so many students repeat this myth because it doesn't take much to demolish it. Here's how to blow it up.

When a classmate says, "There isn't any truth," just ask him, "Oh, is that true?"

Do you see how that works? If he answers, "Sure it's true; I said it, didn't I?" you say, "Then you *admit* that something is true. So why go on denying it?" But if instead he answers, "Of course it's not true because nothing is," then you say, "Well, if it's *not* true that there *isn't* truth, then it *is* true that there *is* truth. So why not just fess up?" Either way, you've got him. He's like one of those cartoon characters that hovers in the air for a few moments after running off the cliff because he hasn't realized yet that nothing is holding him up.

Most of the time, when students say, "There isn't any truth," they don't really mean it anyway. What they're usually trying to say is that life has no meaning or purpose. Most students feel that way sometimes, especially when things are going badly. College can be a friendly and encouraging place, but it can also be a lonely and disheartening one.

Feelings shouldn't be ignored, but they can also be misleading. If you feel as though life has no meaning, ask yourself, "What could give it meaning?"

Couldn't God?

You say He could?

Then how do you know He hasn't?

Myth Number Five: Maybe truth exists, but we can't find it.

Didn't we just go through this? Well, here we go again. Saying that we can't find any truth is just as silly as saying there isn't any to find. If someone says, "We can't find any truth," just ask him, "Oh, is that true?" Maybe he'll answer, "Sing it, brother! That's the way it is!" In that case you say, "If you think *you've* found a truth, then how do you know *I* can't find one?" But maybe instead he'll answer, "How should *I* know whether what I said is true? Weren't you listening?" In that case you say, "If you *don't* know that truth can't be found, then maybe it *can* be found—so why should I listen to *you?*" Either way you've got him. If the last guy was Wile E. Coyote, then this one is Elmer Fudd.

Just as most people don't mean it when they say there isn't any truth, most people don't mean it when they say that it might exist but can't be found. What they're usually trying to say is that it can't be found with *certainty*—that no matter

Pilate Fell for Myth Number Five

What did Pilate mean by his "What is truth?" He seems to have been implying a doctrine fashionable in his time—the lie of the skeptic bound hand and foot in despair, who rather than face his own sins will even doubt his own reality. . . .

—JOY DAVIDMAN, *SMOKE ON THE MOUNTAIN: AN INTERPRETATION OF THE TEN COMMANDMENTS*[2]

what someone thinks, someone can always *doubt*. That's true, but so what?

Not all doubts are reasonable, and some are downright silly. "I think I'm reading a book, but maybe I'm only hallucinating, so I won't bother to finish the chapter." Is that reasonable? "I think I have a daughter, but maybe she and I are just characters in somebody's novel, so I guess there's no point in picking her up from school." Does that make sense?

Our lives shouldn't be based on what can't be doubted, but on what we have the best reasons to believe. All other ways lead to insanity.

Myth Number Six: Maybe we can find out some truth, but not about the biggest and most important things.

When pressed, very few people say they can't find out *any* truth. For instance, not many call it impossible to find out how much the newspaper costs or whether a fish is fresh. People who say we can't find out the truth are usually thinking of greater and more important truths—truths like what's right and wrong or what God is like. The tiny truths they think they can find; it's only the big ones they think they can't. Now that raises an interesting question. Big elephants aren't harder to find than mice. Big lies aren't harder to find than fibs. So why should big truths be harder to find than small ones?

I don't think they are. In fact I think some of the *biggest* truths are the *easiest* to find, because God has provided help. Let's begin with the first of the two big things I just mentioned—what's right and wrong. Do you remember the following story from chapter 4?

> "Morals are all relative anyway," said Tom. "How do we even know that murder is wrong?" The question was a smokescreen, and Frank knew it was. Every human alive knows that murder is wrong; some just pretend they don't.
> So Frank asked, "Are you in *real doubt* that murder is wrong?"
> Tom's first response was evasive: "Many people might say it was all right."
> "But I'm not asking other people," pressed Frank. "Are you at this moment in any real doubt about murder being wrong for everyone?"
> There was a long silence. "No," Tom admitted. "No, I'm not."
> "Good," Frank answered. "Then we don't have to waste time on morals being relative. Let's talk about something you *really are* in doubt about." A few moments passed as Tom realized that his smokescreen, his "cover," had been blown away—then he agreed.

Although I didn't tell you the first time you read the story, this was a real conversation. "Tom" was a student, and "Frank" was a fellow teacher. You see, "Frank" knew what Paul teaches in Romans 2:14-15: God has written the basics of the moral law on the human heart, so even if we tell ourselves we don't know them, we really do. Not many verses earlier, in Romans 1:18-20, Paul says it's the same with the second big thing I mentioned—the basics of what God Himself is like. Deep down, when people look at the things God has made, they recognize His signature. When they look at the world of nature, they can't help but realize it was made by a powerful God, eternal and invisible. That's not all they need to know for salvation, but it's a mighty big hint. The problem is that they hold down their own knowledge. I remember how frustrated I was as an atheist because I was grateful for life even though I was determined to believe that there wasn't anyone to be grateful *to*. I held on to my atheism not because of the evidence, but in spite of it.

For the *Really* Skeptical
Why Should Anyone Believe Anything at All?[3]
—James W. Sire

"Wait a second," says the skeptic. "Where do you get off calling your intuitions *evidence?* I admit you can offer evidence about everyday issues like whether the potato salad is tainted and about scientific issues like whether Darwinian evolution is a fact—we spoke about those before. But you can't offer evidence about moral or religious issues. The reason is simple: There isn't any."

There isn't, eh? Let's try that claim out. How about the moral issue of whether abortion really takes a unique human life? Unborn babies grow and develop, their DNA is different from that of their mothers and fathers, and it's human DNA, not dog or monkey DNA. I'd call that evidence of a unique human life—wouldn't you?

And how about the religious issue of whether Jesus was really God? A man who says he's God is either a lunatic, a scoundrel, or God, but Jesus didn't speak or act like a lunatic or a scoundrel. I'd call that evidence for the third alternative. What other alternative is left?

There's plenty of evidence about the big things. Skeptics just don't want to look.

Relativist Myths

Myth Number Seven: Truth is whatever you sincerely believe.

Can you make something true just by thinking it? What an astonishing power! If you sincerely believe you're a large Diet Coke, will you be one? If you sincerely believe the onion rings are fries, will they be fries? In that

Truth

The LORD is near to all who call on him, to all who call on him in truth.

—PSALM **145:18**

Jesus answered, "I am the way and the truth and the life. No one comes to the Father except through me."

—JOHN **14:6**

Stand firm, then, with the belt of truth buckled around your waist.

—EPHESIANS **6:14**

Do your best to present yourself to God as one approved, a workman who does not need to be ashamed and who correctly handles the word of truth.

—2 TIMOTHY **2:15**

case you must be a mighty magician. I'd like to meet you—if nobody drinks you first!

Now here's something odd. Nobody outside the mental hospitals falls for the "truth is whatever you sincerely believe" gimmick when the subject is Diet Coke or fries, yet many students fall for it when the subject turns to the big, important things we were talking about a few minutes ago. Let me tell you, if your magic doesn't work on fries or Diet Coke, you can be sure it won't work on right and wrong and God!

The fact that we aren't magicians isn't the only problem with the sincerity myth. Another is that it leads to inconsistencies. You sincerely say the window's open; I sincerely say it's not. If you're right, I'm wrong, and if I'm right, you're wrong. Sincerity can't change that. But the sincerity myth says it can. It says that since we're both sincere, we must both be right. You're right, so the window is open; but I'm right too, so it's not. Some sincerists try to get out of jams like this by using the words "for me" and "for you." Of course, saying the window is open for you but closed for me doesn't help a bit. If it's open, it's open for us both, and if it's closed, it's closed for us both. But sincerists don't waste *for me* and *for you* on little things like windows. As before, they save their myth for big things like right and wrong and God.

Here's the sort of thing I mean. Two sincerists are having lunch. The first one says, "I sincerely believe that God is my inner self," and the second replies, "I sincerely believe that God is tuna fish." The first returns, "Then 'God is tuna fish' is true for you, but 'God is my inner self' is true for me." They cheerfully agree. Later the same two sincerists are having dinner. The first one says, "I sincerely believe that infanticide is right," and the second replies, "I sincerely believe that infanticide is wrong." The first returns, "Then 'infanticide is wrong' is true for you, but 'infanticide is right' is true for me." They smile and eat their salads.

I'm being silly, but not nearly as silly as you think. True, nobody on campus thinks God is tuna fish, but many a student thinks God is his inner self, and considers his sincerity enough to make it so. As to infanticide—you'd be surprised how many people on campus think an unborn baby isn't human unless the mother sincerely believes he is. If the sincerity of her belief could make all that difference for unborn babies, why couldn't it for born ones too? In fact, some pro-abortion people already think this way. Biochemist James Watson *sincerely believes* that babies should not be considered alive for three days after they're born.[4] Some people have sincerely suggested that three days are too few—they want thirty.

The problem is that sincerity doesn't make anything true, and it doesn't make anything true *just for you,* either. In fact, there is no truth *just for you.* Truth is for everyone. We just have to share it.

Myth Number Eight: Truth is whatever people accept— or whatever you can get them to swallow.

This myth wears many disguises. If you're a Christian, perhaps a fellow student will scoff at your beliefs by calling them "old-fashioned," "archaic," or "obsolete." What he means is "People around here *don't accept them* anymore, and that's all it takes to make them false." Put in plain words, the claim is ridiculous. Of course, that's why he doesn't use plain words!

Your teachers may dress the myth in even fancier clothing. In political science class you might hear about "communitarianism."

Just in Case You Were Wondering
Each human cell has 46 chromosomes; each dog cell, 60. If all of the DNA in one of your cells were unraveled, it would make a string about six feet long.

This is the idea that there aren't any standards of truth but the ones your community agrees to. In sociology class you might hear about the "social construction of reality." This is the idea that things are only real, or true, if your society accepts that they are. In philosophy class you may hear about the "consensus theory of truth." Consensus is agreement, so if someone says he believes the consensus theory, he too is telling you that agreement makes things true.

As you can see, these are all pretty much the same idea. When people try them out on me, I like to reply: "Some people don't accept your theory that truth is agreement. But that means we *don't* have agreement that truth is agreement. So doesn't your theory call *itself* false?" You might try the question yourself, just to see how it makes people squirm.

The idea that truth is whatever you can get people to swallow has a superficial appeal because there really are *some* cases where agreement makes a thing true. The English agree that motorists on English streets should drive on the left—and so they should. The Americans agree that an American foot has twelve inches—and so it does. But there are also cases where no amount of agreement can make a thing true. Vikings agreed that the earth was flat. Did that mean it was? Nazis agreed that Jews should be killed. Did that mean they should have been? People on the modern campus reply, "But *we* don't think that the earth is flat or that Jews should be killed." No, they don't, but they consider their agreement enough to make some equally strange things true—for instance, that men may have sex with men or that women may have sex with women.

The flaw in the notion that truth is whatever you can get people to swallow is so easy to spot that you may be asking, "Why doesn't everybody see it?" The Christian philosopher Alvin Plantinga suggests one reason:

> One thing about this way of thinking: It has great possibilities when it comes to your having done something wrong. Lie about it; and if you are successful (if you get your peers to let you get away with saying that you didn't do it) then it will be true that you didn't do it and in fact you won't have done it; as an added bonus you won't even have lied about it![6]

I think that's a big part of the answer. Swallowism isn't true, but for putting a troubled conscience to sleep, nothing can beat it.

Myth Number Nine: Truth is whatever works.

Fourteen or fifteen years ago I told my brother that I'd returned from atheism to Christianity. He said, "Well, if it works for you, fine." I was puzzled by his statement then, and I'm puzzled by it now.

In the first place, whether something works for someone is merely personal, like whether he believes it sincerely. The "something" might work for him but not for me. By contrast, whether the claims of Christ are true is more than merely personal. Like "the earth is round" or "heavy objects have more mass than lighter ones," if His claims are true for anyone, they're true for everyone.

Besides, I don't know what it means for faith in Jesus to work for someone. Does it give him comfort? Does it get him a job? Does it make him honest? None of these things can prove a belief is true.

Beforehand, I Liked Myself

"Beforehand, I liked myself. I had never entertained the idea of abortion. But the minute that needle went through my abdomen, I hated it, because I knew it could not be reversed. I wanted to scream, 'Don't do this to me!'"

—NancyJo Mann[5]

Atheism is false, but it might give me comfort if I'm angry enough at God. Astrology is bunk, but it might get me a job with the newspaper if I know how to cast a horoscope. There aren't any fairies, but thinking there are might make me honest if I'm afraid they're watching to see if I lie.

The myth that truth is whatever works takes two forms at college: one in the classroom and another in campus social life. In the classroom it takes the form of a philosophical theory called "pragmatism," which happens to be enjoying a fad at the moment. Pragmatism confuses many students, but if you keep in mind the points you've read in the last two paragraphs, you'll be okay. Just remember that what works for one person may not work for another; that what works in one *way* may not work in another; and most important, that no matter which way of working you have in mind, something can work and still be wrong. To ask whether a statement is true isn't to ask whether it works, but whether it's *accurate,* whether it's *factual,* whether *what it says is so.* Only the whiteness of snow gives truth to the statement "Snow is white"; only the Lordship of Jesus gives truth to the statement "Jesus is Lord."

In campus social life the myth that truth is whatever works takes a different form—the form of a conversation stopper. You may have a friend who used to have ideals but now cares for nothing but money. Is that really all that matters? "Hey, it works for me." Another friend gets bombed every weekend and has started to drink on the weekdays too. Does it really make sense to destroy himself? "Hey, it works for me." Still another friend has had two abortions and sleeps with every man she meets. Can this really be the way she ought to live? "Hey, it works for me." Be patient with your friends, but recognize their slogan for what it is—not a way to find the truth, but a wall to keep truth out.

Jesus was right: The truth shall set you free. But the myth of "whatever works" can only keep you in chains.

WAR

This chapter may have been a challenge, so let's take a quick last look at the ground we've covered.

First, thinking you know the truth isn't arrogant or intolerant; arrogance comes from having the wrong convictions about how to treat people who don't share it with you.

Second, the whole point of searching for truth is to find it; saying the important thing in life isn't having truth but searching for it is like saying the important thing in sickness isn't getting well but seeing doctors.

Third, reasoning depends on faith; falsely placed faith will keep you from the truth, but rightly placed faith will help you find it.

Fourth, it doesn't make sense that there is no truth because then it wouldn't even be true that there isn't.

Fifth, it doesn't make sense to claim truth can't be found because to claim anything at all is to imply that the claim is true.

Sixth, the biggest and most important truths aren't harder to find than the little ones; in fact they're easier because God has provided help.

Seventh, truth isn't whatever you sincerely believe; only a mighty magician could make something true just by thinking it.

Eighth, popular agreement doesn't make a statement true; people have been swallowing nonsense since the world began.

Ninth, the slogan that truth is whatever works isn't a pathway to the truth; it's a wall to keep it out.

Why must all this be so hard? Because you're going into war. I don't mean a war of bombs and bullets and ballistic missiles. I mean a much more fiery, deadly war of errors and sins and temptations—of mind-bombs, soul-bullets, and spiritual powers at great heights. You see, according to the Bible it's not just a coincidence that the world keeps going wrong. The Prince of Deceptions launches lies against us, and the world finds them more attractive than the truth. Our eyes don't see as the angels do, but whenever someone accepts one of the Enemy's myths it must look to them like a warhead exploding in his heart, strewing death and destruction in all directions.

For believers, there's nothing to be afraid of because the armor of God is stronger than the weapons of the Enemy. *But you have to strap it on.*

One more thing. Do you notice anything missing from Paul's description of the armor of God in Ephesians 6:10-18? He mentions the belt of truth, the breastplate of righteousness, and the footguards of readiness to spread the gospel. Then he mentions the shield of faith, the helmet of salvation, and the sword of the Spirit, which is the Word of God. Lacing everything together is prayer. But all of this armor is for your front. Paul mentions no armor for your back.

Why is that? Because God does not intend that you ever turn your back to the foe. Wear your armor and advance when you can; stand when you must, but never retreat. Remember this, and you'll always be victorious.

No Armor for His Back

"But now in this Valley of Humiliation poor Christian was hard put to it; for he had gone but a little way before he espied a foul fiend coming over the field to meet him; his name is Apollyon. Then did Christian begin to be afraid, and to cast in his mind whether to go back or to stand his ground. But he considered again that he had no armour for his back; and therefore thought that to turn the back to him might give him the greater advantage with ease to pierce him with his darts. Therefore he resolved to venture and stand his ground; for, thought he, had I no more in mine eye than the saving of my life, it would be the best way to stand."

JOHN BUNYAN, *THE PILGRIM'S PROGRESS* (1678)

Chapter 6

MYTHS ABOUT LOVE AND SEX

MISERY

Sitting across from me in the counseling room was a young man wild with feelings for which he had no name. Some weeks earlier he had taken his girlfriend for an abortion. It all seemed okay at the time. Everyone else said so too. But then, some time later, when his grandfather died, he began to reflect about death. On the way home from the funeral it hit him: He had killed his baby. That's when the world caved in on him. Some friends, afraid of what he might do to himself, had called the Crisis Pregnancy Center, and the Center called me. Because no men's recovery groups were meeting, I was asked to work with him one-on-one. By then he was desperate to talk.

It's true that he was a little unusual. With most men, the impact of abortion takes longer to sink in, they're less willing to talk about it, and they tend to feel it differently than he did—for example as a diminished sense of manhood. But there he was, flesh and blood, a living testimony that the notion that sex has no consequences is a myth.

Our supposedly enlightened age is awash in myths about sex and love. This chapter covers *general myths* (the ones men and women are equally likely to fall for), *girl myths* (the ones women are more likely to fall for), and *guy myths* (the ones men are more likely to fall for). I'll spend almost the same amount of time on general and girl myths, but on guy myths my comments will be about fifty percent longer because guys take more convincing.

Need Help? Need Answers?

For immediate practical help for someone in a crisis pregnancy, call Care Net at 1-800-395-HELP.

For help holding your own in the abortion debate, check out Randy Alcorn, *Pro Life Answers to Pro Choice Arguments*.[1]

General Myths

Myth Number One: Love is a feeling, and sex is the adult way to express it.

Have you ever wondered why when people get married, they *promise* to love each other until death? Think about it. Feelings change. You can't promise to have a feeling. So if love is a feeling, the marriage vow makes no sense at all. But the vow does make sense because love is *not* a feeling. What is it, then? *Love is a commitment of the will to the true good of another person.* Of course, people who love each other usually do have strong feelings too, but you can have those feelings without having love. Love, let me repeat, is a commitment of the will to the true good of another person.

Now the *outward expression and seal* of a commitment of the will is a binding promise. So the adult way to express love is to *enter into* a binding promise—and that's what we call marriage. "If you really loved me," some people say, "you'd do it with me." Baloney. If he really loved you, he wouldn't demand it. If she really loved you, she wouldn't either.

Myth Number Two: Sex is just like everything else; in order to make wise choices about it, you have to experience it.

Is it really true of "everything else" that to make wise choices about it, you have to experience it? Well, it's certainly true that there are *some* things you can't decide about from the outside. You need inside knowledge. As a Christian, for example, I've found that in order to know Jesus Christ you have to just trust Him; there's no experiment you can perform, no test to subject Him to, except trust itself.

But other things in this life aren't like that at all. Drug addiction is one; suicide is another. Nobody would say that you have to be a drug addict to become wise about drugs; nobody would say that you have to commit suicide in order to find out whether it's a good idea. In fact, in these cases experience is the one thing that *keeps* you from being able to choose wisely about them. Over the centuries, the human race has discovered quite a number of cases like this—behaviors that impair instead of enhance the ability to choose wisely, experiences that subtract from rather than add to understanding. That's one of the reasons they've been called sins and vices, and that people have been warned away from them instead of encouraged to try them.

Sex outside of marriage is one of these cases. If you really want to understand it, you have to stay away from it. If you plunge right into it, you'll no longer understand it. The only way to understand sex from the *inside* is to understand it from inside marriage.

Myth Number Three: Without sex, you'll never know whether you're compatible with someone; without living together, you'll never know whether a marriage between you would work.

If it were really true that living together is a trial of marriage, then divorces would be more common among couples who hadn't first lived together than among couples who had. Actually, just the opposite is true: Divorces are more common among couples who have lived together first than among couples who haven't. The reason isn't hard to find. The very essence of marriage is having a binding commitment. The very essence of living together is having *no* binding commitment. That's why living together can't be a trial for marriage, because in everything that matters the two conditions are opposites. And that's why not having a binding commitment is less like training for marriage than like training for divorce.

What about the idea that you need to find out whether you're sexually compatible? Sexual compatibility is a truly crazy idea. Nobody is born with a particular style in bed; people *learn* to have sex. Anyone can learn in a marriage: there's all the time in the world, you're completely safe, and mistakes are just funny because you love each other. After twenty-five years of marriage I'm still learning new things. On the other hand, *no one* can properly learn to have sex *outside* a marriage: there isn't any time, you have no security in the relationship, and mistakes are humiliating because—let's face it—you're on an audition. All you can do in that sort of relationship is pick up a couple of sexual "habits." When unmarried people chatter about sexual compatibility, what they mean is that the sexual habits that the *woman* picked up in sleeping with her previous *men* just happen

Is Everybody *Really* Doing It?

Sometimes I think I'm weird because I want to wait to have sex, but hearing about this survey and finding out that there are so many people on this campus [UCLA] who aren't having sex makes me feel better.

—"Julie," a 19-year-old sociology student

I know lots of other people who aren't having sex. I have a V-Club going with a bunch of people in my dorm. . . . It's hard being a virgin if you don't want to be, but it's pretty easy to remain one if you want to. No one makes me feel like I have to have sex to be cool or popular. I make the rules for me.

—"Tom," a 20-year-old communications studies student

I don't think everybody's having sex. I have lots of friends who are virgins.

—"Lee," a political science student

I want to wait until I get married to have sex. It has to do with my upbringing as a Catholic and my belief in my faith.

—"Kelly," a 21-year-old biology student[2]

to resemble the sexual habits that the *man* picked up in sleeping with his previous *women*. Wouldn't it be more fun and more exciting to learn to make love just with each other, completely from scratch, in the security of a marriage relationship?

GIRL MYTHS
Myth Number Four: Sex outside marriage is romantic.
Women, how romantic is it to stand buck-naked in front of a man who hasn't committed his life to you? The only time it's romantic to be completely vulnerable to a man is when you know you're absolutely safe with him: He isn't going to give you a disease, he isn't going to get you pregnant and then tell you to have an abortion, he isn't going to be sleeping with other women, he isn't going to leave you—all because he cares more about what's truly good for you than he cares about himself. Yes, being vulnerable to a man in *that* case really is romantic. But the name of that case is marriage. Only marriage can offer that kind of romance; only marriage can offer that kind of excitement.

The Myth of Trial Marriage
Couples who live together before they marry have divorce rates 50 to 100 percent higher than couples who don't. In a Canadian study of couples married less than 10 years, the divorce rate was 31 percent for those who lived together first, but only 14 percent for those who didn't. Studies also show that couples who lived together before marriage quarrel more, communicate less, separate more often, seek more counseling, and are more likely to have extramarital affairs. They have more problems with drugs and alcohol, and regard marriage as a less important part of their lives.

Cohabiting couples report higher rates of depression and lower rates of sexual satisfaction than married couples. Their rates of violence are twice as high, and their rates of severe violence five times as high. In three out of four live-in relationships, at least one partner reports having thought the relationship was in trouble over the past year. This is twice the rate for otherwise similar married couples.

—GLENN T. STANTON, *WHY MARRIAGE MATTERS*[3]

Men, this is for you too. Let's be honest, can we? The truth is that many us are even more romantic than women are, but in a different way. As the historians can tell you, *we* were the ones who invented the romantic ideal of knighthood.

Now let's turn the tables: How romantic is it to *put* a woman in the position of standing buck-naked in front of you when you haven't committed your life to her? For that matter, how romantic is it to get her pregnant? Or to give her a disease? If that's what you're doing, aren't you really treating her like a prostitute, not a lover? There's a difference between being a "john" and being a man. The knight honors, adores, and protects his lady; he doesn't *use* her.

Myth Number Five: Sex outside marriage holds relationships together.

It's true that you can often get a man to hang around for a while by giving him sex. The mistake lies in thinking that you can get him to *stay* around by giving him sex. There are four pitfalls along this path.

First, sex outside of marriage tends to make relationships worse, not better. You used to see movies together, you used to see friends together, you used to have endless conversations; now all you do is have sex. You have it more and more but enjoy it less and less because it's *taking the place* of the relationship instead of enriching it the way it would in marriage.

Second, although it may be politically incorrect to say so, a man will never set a higher value on you than you set on yourself. He might have sex with a woman who tumbles into bed easily, but he's not likely to marry a woman who tumbles into bed easily. Why should he? He'd always be wondering who you might tumble into bed with next. So do you really want to be his practice doll?

Third, the more you give him sex, the more you'll expect from the relationship because that's how most woman are made. The problem is that most men aren't. The greater your expectations, the more he'll resent them because, outside marriage, he doesn't have any commitment.

Fourth, variety is typically more intriguing to men than it is to women. I know it isn't fashionable to say that either, but it's true. So the more you give your boyfriend sex, the sooner he'll get bored and find someone else to sleep with. Isn't that a problem in marriage, too? No. Marriage is different because it provides a deeper variety that doesn't depend on changing beds. I'll say more about that when I discuss Myth Number Nine.

Myth Number Six: Sex outside of marriage is a sign of commitment.

We said before that love is a commitment of the will to the true good of another person, but we also said that its *seal* is the binding promises of marriage. Before that point, everything is reversible, even engagement. So how can you tell whether you've got a commitment? Simple. If you're married, you have one. If you're not married, you don't. Do you have a boyfriend who says he's committed to you but he's just not ready for marriage? He's lying. The whole point of not marrying is to avoid commitment. How can a person be commit*ted* to you, yet reject a commit*ment* to you? So sex outside of marriage isn't a sign of commitment; it's a sign that he's gotten his way.

GUY MYTHS

Myth Number Seven: Sex is a physical need, and physical needs can't be wrong.

One of the great secrets of living is that there is a difference between a *want* and a *need*. A want is merely a desire; a need is something life requires. For example, I *need* food, but I only *want* a Milky Way bar. Without food I'll die, but without a Milky Way bar I'll only be disappointed. The problem with myth number seven is that it confuses these two things. It says that sex is a physical need, but in reality sex is only a physical want. Nobody dies from not having sex.

True, some guys *act* like they'll die without it. But let's be honest. The main reason for acting like that is to make your girlfriend feel sorry for you so she'll give in. The only other reason I can think of is that you feel sorry for yourself. Now don't get me wrong: I understand why you feel sorry for yourself. If you've been having sex just to relieve desire, you're in the same sad predicament as the man who's been scratching to relieve the itch of a bug bite. Yes, scratching relieves the itch for a moment, but the more you scratch, the sooner the itch comes back, even stronger than it was before. Pretty soon you're caught in a circle of itching and scratching, itching and scratching, and instead of being satisfied, you're more frustrated than before you began. You start itching all over. All you can think about is where you're going to get the next scratch. When you meet a woman, the only thing that matters to you is whether she's got long fingernails!

The only way out of this vicious cycle is to go cold turkey. It isn't easy, but the alternative is worse. Don't have sex just to relieve desire; wait until marriage, where having sex is part of making love.

Myth Number Eight: Sex is for pleasure, and pleasure can't be wrong.

Why in the world would anyone think that pleasure can't be wrong? People get pleasure in all sorts of wrong ways: from listening in on other people's conversations, from getting stupid on drugs, from driving at high speeds on busy highways — why, some people even get pleasure from inflicting pain on others. Now I know what some of you are thinking. You're thinking that the pleasure of sex outside of marriage is different because sex outside marriage doesn't hurt anybody. If you're thinking that, I've got two things to say to you.

The first is: Where have you been for the last few pages? Haven't you been listening? I don't know how much clearer I can make it that by having sex outside of marriage you're wrecking your relationship, ruining romance, dishonoring your partner, and in general messing up your life and hers.

The second is: Where have you been for the last *eighteen years?* AIDS, herpes, chlamydia, syphilis, gonorrhea, genital warts, and more than a dozen other sexually transmitted diseases, most of which used to be rare, are ravaging the population. One and a half million abortions are performed in this country every year. The rate of illegitimate births is climbing so fast that in some places in this country more babies are born outside of marriage than within it. Don't you think it's time to decommission the slogan that sex outside of marriage doesn't hurt anybody?

The second problem with the idea of living for pleasure is this. Have you ever heard of the Hedonistic Paradox? A hedonist is a person whose goal in life is pleasure. The Hedonistic Paradox is that if you chase pleasure, it flies away; if you pursue it for its own sake, after a while you can't get any of it at all! We could argue all day and night about *why* this is true. The point is that it *is* true. If you live for pleasure, you won't have any. Now the *name* "Hedonistic Paradox" comes from the philosophers. But you don't have to go to the philosophers to hear about it. When I was in high school, Mick Jagger of the Rolling Stones used to sing a song called "I Can't Get No Satisfaction," and very few of us had difficulty figuring out what kind of satisfaction he was probably talking about. Here's the bottom line: The only way you can get pleasure, sexual or any other kind, is to get it as a byproduct of pursuing something else— like the true good of another person. So: Do you want true and lasting pleasure? Then you have to stop *chasing* pleasure. Start pursuing *love*. Wait for marriage. It's your only chance.

Freedom

Freedom didn't occur overnight. The times I fell back into my sin were too numerous to count. Yet each time I did fall I got back up and turned to God. Continuing in God means not giving up. It means really wanting to put God first and the world behind us. "When Jesus saw him lying there and learned that he had been in this condition for a long time, he asked him, 'Do you want to get well?'" (John 5:6). I never realized it until after the facts, but I didn't have complete freedom over sexual sin until I truly wanted it.

—CLAY BROWN, "SET FREE TO FOLLOW CHRIST: FREEDOM FROM PORNOGRAPHY." YOU CAN READ THE REST OF HIS STORY AT http://www.leaderu.com/common/porn.html.[4]

Myth Number Nine: Marriage is boring because there isn't any variety.

Now I've already said that guys are more interested in variety than girls are. However, there are two kinds of variety: superficial variety and deep variety. By superficial variety I mean experiencing one woman after another, but never getting past their surfaces. By deep variety I mean experiencing depth after depth of the *same* woman, not only the surface but every other level of her personality. A whole other person, someone who just *isn't you,* is an amazing thing, always new, always surprising. This relationship provides endless variety, but inside the unity of a single soul who loves you. The first kind of variety is like getting your feet wet in fifteen wading pools in one day. The second kind is like swimming in the ocean. I'd rather swim in the ocean, wouldn't you?

Now maybe you're thinking you don't have to choose. Maybe you're thinking that you can have superficial variety for a few years and still enjoy deep variety when you get married; that you can try out all the wading pools now and still swim in the ocean later. Sorry, it doesn't work that way. The problem is that changing from bed to bed eventually destroys the very *ability* to experience the depths of another person. Here's a way to think of what I'm talking about. You've used sticky tape, right? It's great for sealing boxes and gluing things together. But you know, you have to be careful when you use it. A fresh piece of tape sticks to whatever it touches, whether you want it to or not. Tape can't help it; *that's what it's for.* But if you don't like where the tape is sticking and you try to rip it loose, there's going to be damage. The package will tear. And when you do get the tape loose it isn't as sticky as it was before. Press it on and pull it loose from one thing after another, and eventually it won't stick to anything at all.

Your sexuality is like that, but emotionally and spiritually rather than physically. Just as a fresh piece of tape sticks to *what*ever it touches, the first time in your life you use your sexuality you're going to stick to *who*ever it touches. Sex can't help it; *that's what it's for.* But if you don't like who you're sticking to and you try to rip yourself loose, there's going to be damage. Something in your heart will tear, and something will tear in the other person too. And when you do get yourself loose, your sexuality won't be as sticky as it was before. Press it on and pull it loose from one person after another, and eventually it won't stick to anyone at all. You'll sleep with various partners as you have before, but they'll seem like strangers to you. You just won't feel anything. You'll have destroyed your capacity for intimacy.

Now some of you guys agree with the reply I've just given to the superficial-variety-now-deep-variety-later objection, but you have a different objection. You understand the difference between the two kinds of variety, and you understand that going in for the superficial kind destroys the capacity for the deep kind. You're thinking to yourself: "Okay, I want the deep kind. I don't want a dozen wading pools, I want the ocean. I don't want the surface of a dozen women, I want depth after depth of the same woman." But you're also thinking, "I want to keep my options open. I'm for intimacy, but I'm not for promises. I'm for one partner, but I'm not for marriage."

Is that your thought? If so, you may as well forget it. Outside of marriage there's not a chance for that kind of intimacy. You may as well look for the ocean on the moon. Why is that? The reason is a great secret, although it shouldn't be.

You want to keep your options open, but intimacy requires throwing them away.

Did you hear that? Let me say it again. You want to keep your options open, but intimacy requires throwing them away. That's why lovers have to be married, and that's why marriage has to be permanent. If you and your girlfriend haven't given your lives to each other for good, you'll always be holding back from each other, whether you know it or not. In fact, you'd be crazy not to. Why should you open all your treasures to someone who might leave you? Why should she? But "holding back" is another way of saying you're not swimming in the ocean after all. You may reach for her depths, but you'll only bruise your heart on the wading pool floor. You may think you're swimming in the ocean because you can't feel the bottom. But that's only because you're not really reaching for it, and neither is she.

Procrastination

O Lord, give me chastity and continence, but not yet.

—Saint Augustine[5]

NOT FOR NOTHING

Just so there can be no misunderstanding, let me review what I've said in this chapter.

First, love isn't a feeling; it's a commitment of the will to the true good of another person. That means that its adult expression isn't sex, but the binding promises of marriage.

Second, sex outside of marriage doesn't help you understand sex better so that you can make wise choices about it; in fact it makes your understanding of sex worse so that wise choices are harder.

Third, having sex with another person tells you nothing about whether the two of you are compatible, and living together tells you nothing about whether a marriage between you would work.

Fourth, sex outside of marriage isn't romantic; in fact it is the very opposite of romantic.

Fifth, sex outside of marriage doesn't hold relationships together; it contributes to their decay.

Sixth, sex outside of marriage isn't a sign of commitment; it's a sign that someone is getting what he wants.

Seventh, the desire for sex is not a need but a want, and scratching whenever you itch will merely start a vicious cycle.

Eighth, pleasures can be bad as well as good; besides, sex outside of marriage doesn't bring lasting pleasure—rather it murders pleasure.

Ninth, it isn't marriage that's boring, it's promiscuity that's boring; and the excitement of marital intimacy just can't be found by playing house.

Before I close the chapter, let me give you something deeper to think about. Why did God make two different sexes anyway? He didn't have to. There are other ways to arrange for reproduction, you know. God could have arranged for us to bud or to divide. Instead, He set up a complicated system in which making new little human beings depends on cooperation between two different kinds of big ones. And that isn't the only thing that draws the sexes together. Male and female are like hand and glove; each sex feels incomplete and *longs* for the other. God could have made a single self-sufficient sex that felt perfectly complete and didn't long for anybody, but He didn't. Why not?

Do you know what I think? I think God made us male and female because we *need* to long for each other. It's not good not to long for someone; it's not good to be absorbed in yourself. Somehow, each of us needs to get out of self. With the help of God's grace, the marriage of a man and woman can make that happen. Solitary sex can't do that; it sinks a person more deeply in the self. Homosexual sex can't do that; it sinks him into a looking-glass idol of the self. Casual sex can't do that; it merely uses the other for the purposes of the self.

But a marriage with Christ at the center of it pulls you right out of yourself. It teaches each partner, the husband and the wife, to forget about self for a while in care and sacrifice for the other. We come to ourselves by losing ourselves.

And you know what? There's an even deeper mystery. Intimate and profound as it is, marriage to a human "other" is just a hint, a glimpse, a foretaste, of an even *more* intimate, even *more* profound union with Someone who is even *more* "other." I'm talking about the spiritual union with God Himself, which is promised to every Christian in heaven. The Bible compares heaven to a wedding feast. So if anyone asks you, you can tell him you're engaged.

Chapter 7

Myths About Politics

Flare-Up

Not long ago on my own campus, several hundred liberal students occupied a law school building to protest a conservative professor's statements against racial preferences in admissions—policies which give some races more favorable treatment in admissions than others. Racial preferences were a hot issue because the law school had previously been ordered by a federal court to stop using them.[1] What got the professor in trouble was his statement that families in some ethnic groups give greater emphasis to academic study than families in others. While one side called this remark a fair-minded statement of fact, the other called it a racist stereotype. Tempers flared, and soon people were taking over the building and the school was all over the nightly news.

All right, so some campuses are politically charged. What does *that* have to do with staying Christian in politics? It only takes three steps to explain.

Step one: As you see from the story, politics deals with basic issues of right and wrong.

Step two: As even a glance at the Bible will show, God has plenty to say about right and wrong.

Step three: When people don't like what God says about right and wrong (or what they *think* He says about right and wrong), they tend to make a god of their own ideas. Their ideologies become substitute religions. Then they've got a problem because God will have no other gods before Him.

You may think that if you're not interested in politics, it won't affect your thinking. What I find is just the opposite. Politically apathetic students are even *more* influenced by the political ideas raining down on them because they aren't thinking about them critically. They aren't taking the trouble to separate the wheat from the chaff.

THE RUNDOWN

This chapter moves faster than the last one because I don't think politics is as hard to think about as sex. The things you'd expect in a civics class are all left out, and if you want to know about the gross national product, you're reading the wrong book.

But this chapter does cover just as many myths as the last one did: political myths. You might hear these myths anywhere—in the classroom, at a student political rally, even among friends in the dorm. But you'll have to listen closely for them because sometimes they hide between the lines. I cover *general myths* (as usual, these are the ones almost anyone might swallow), *liberal myths* (the ones people on the Left are more likely to swallow), and *conservative myths* (the ones people on the Right are more likely to swallow).[2]

If you've already swallowed any of these false ideas, some parts of the chapter may make you angry. That's all right; I don't mind a bit.

All Right, If You Insist
The *gross national product* is the total value of the goods and services produced by a nation's inhabitants in a year.

GENERAL MYTHS

Myth Number One: God belongs to your party.

A big mistake many Christian students make in politics is that they forget to seek *God's* will and instead expect Him to carry out *their* will. Some Democrats think God is a Democrat; some Republicans think He is a Republican. Some liberals think He is a liberal; some conservatives think He is a conservative. They expect God to support every detail of political programs in which He wasn't consulted.

Sometimes this attitude seems merely silly, as in the case of the speaker who prays at a big political rally, "God, lead *your party* to victory." But the attitude can also lead into blasphemy. An especially common case on campus is that some Christians get sucked into the pro-abortion cause, then ask the very God who makes children in the womb to help them fight for the right to destroy them. What can they be thinking?

We exist to serve God. He doesn't exist to serve us. No country, no political party, no political ideology can own Him. He's the boss.

Myth Number Two: Everyone belongs to himself.

Many people on campus think that human beings make themselves, belong to themselves, and have value in and of themselves. That may sound pretty abstract, but it has practical implications. In politics, if you think you own yourself you'll probably also think you have a right to assisted suicide, a right to abortion, and in general a right to do just as you please—and of course, you'll want the laws to back you up.

The Bible expresses a very different view: that human beings are made by God, belong to Him, and have value because He loves them and they are made in His image. Does this make a difference in politics? It sure does. Take suicide: If God owns us all, then we have a duty to live for Him, not kill ourselves; but for His sake we also owe each other compassion in times of trouble.

Myth Number Three: The ends justify the means.

Many people in politics think it's okay to do anything to achieve their political goals—stuffing ballot boxes, shredding public documents, shaking people down for political contributions, whatever it takes. You might think this view thrives only in places like Washington, DC. Think again, because it lives on campus too! This student cheats to win the student government election; that professor distorts the facts to win supporters to his political cause.

Slipping into political dishonesty is easier than you might think. One little lie leads to another, and pretty soon you're telling whoppers. To soothe your sense of guilt, you lie to yourself, too. Maybe you tell yourself you're not really lying but just "repackaging the facts." Maybe you take up the motto, "You can't make an omelet without breaking a few eggs." Maybe you repeat false philosophies you've heard in the classroom, like, "Acts must be judged by their consequences." Or maybe you just make excuses— "I know the end doesn't *usually* justify the means, *but my case is special.*" Before long you've told so many lies that you can't even remember the truth. Worse yet, people who forget the truth usually go on to forget the *Truth*—and I think you know *Who* I mean!

Finding the Truth again is terribly hard. It's better not to leave Him in the first place.

LIBERAL MYTHS

Myth Number Four: The job of the government is to reform everything.

God assigned some social institutions their own special purposes or jobs. For instance, the family is for raising children and the church is for building up God's kingdom. What about government? Has God assigned that social institution a special purpose too? Yes, government is for punishing those who do wrong and honoring those who do right (1 Peter 2:14). For punishing it uses courts, jails, and armies, and for praising it has things like public memorials and medals of honor. This job of punishing and honoring is called *upholding public justice.*

In this sinful world, it's inevitable that many good things that should happen don't, and that many bad things that shouldn't happen do. Because government is so powerful, many college students think it can be used to make all the good things happen and stop all the bad things from happening. To do this they want government to horn in on the affairs of the *other* social institutions, like family and church. Misusing words, they call *that* upholding public justice. The sad thing is that when government tries to take on jobs that aren't its own, it only makes things worse.

Myth Number Five: Compassion means cheap generosity.

Obviously, Christianity teaches compassion. Many Christian students who get wrapped up in political causes confuse compassion with cheap generosity. How can generosity be cheap? One way is when it is at someone else's expense. It's easy to say that other people should be taxed to help a group you feel sorry for.

Calm down. I'm not telling you whether such spending is good or bad; that's not my point. My point is that you shouldn't kid yourself by calling it compassion. True compassion is when *you* are the one who bears the burden and pays the price. Am I getting through?

Generosity is also cheap when we do what makes us feel good instead of what really helps. It may make you feel good to support big government handouts. But the truth is that *government* can't really help the poor. It really does help if you wash pots and pans in a soup kitchen, spend time with a fatherless little boy, or teach an illiterate woman to read—but only *you* can do that, and it's hard.

The Two Cows Theory of Political and Ecomomic Systems

Feudalism: You have two cows. Your lord takes some of the milk.

Communism: You have two cows. The government takes all the milk.

Bureaucracy: You have two cows. At first the government regulates what you can feed them and when you can milk them. Then it pays you not to milk them. After that it takes both, shoots one, milks the other and pours the milk down the drain. Then it requires you to fill out forms accounting for the missing cows.

Capitalism: You have two cows. You sell one and buy a bull.

Counterculture: Wow, dude, there's like . . . these two cows, man. You got to have some of this milk.[3]

Myth Number Six: Faith and politics should be separate.

Wait a minute, professor! How can you call it a "myth" that religion and politics should be separate? Doesn't the Constitution call for a "wall of separation between church and state"?

Nope! Even when you include the amendments, the Constitution says only three things about religion. First, government isn't allowed to make officeholders pass a religious test; second, it isn't allowed to establish an official church; and third, it isn't allowed to stop anyone from worshiping freely. These three rules are meant to protect your liberty to follow God, not to abolish it. That famous slogan about a "wall of separation" just isn't there.

In 1947 the Supreme Court pointed out that if the line of separation *were* like a "wall," firemen couldn't even put out fires in religious schools, because firemen are government employees![5] That, said the Court, would be ridiculous. The upshot: There is no "wall." If there were, we would have to protest it. Christians are free to act according to their convictions in politics, just as atheists are free to act according to theirs.

What the Constitution Says About Religion

Article VI: "no religious test shall ever be required as a Qualification to any Office or public Trust under the United States."

Amendment I: "Congress shall make no law respecting an establishment of religion, or prohibiting the free exercise thereof."[4]

Meaning: (1) The government is not allowed to make people take a religious test in order to qualify for holding federal office. (2) Congress is not allowed to set up an official national church. (3) Congress is not allowed to stop people from practicing their religions.

CONSERVATIVE MYTHS

Myth Number Seven: The job of the government is to keep everything the same.

Do you remember Chicken Little, the underage birdbrain who thought the sky was falling? Another day, Chicken Little was crying to everyone, "Fire! Fire!" Finally the cow said, "You silly chicken, there's no fire here. Can't you tell?" Seeing that this was true, Chicken Little immediately began to cry, "Flood! Flood!"

Politics is much like that, on campus as well as elsewhere. Many people who escape from the myth that the job of the government is to reform everything merely fall for the opposite myth that the job of the government is to keep everything the same. For example, I've heard it argued that although it was wrong to legalize abortion, it would also be wrong to make it illegal again—*just because people are used to it and wouldn't like the change.* That argument defends a *liberal* injustice with a *conservative* myth. Common sense tells you that some things should be changed and others shouldn't.

Myth Number Eight: Wealth is a measure of moral virtue.

Just as some people have a hard time understanding what compassion really is, others have a hard time understanding why compassion is important in the first place. Some of my students tell me that government handouts have rewarded laziness and dependency. Generally, I think that's true. But sometimes they go on to suggest that all of the needy are lazy and dependent and that all of the wealthy have achieved their wealth through virtue and hard work. That's not true at all.

In fact, Jesus said that it's harder for a rich man to enter the kingdom than for a camel to pass through the eye of a needle (Luke 6:20; Luke 18:24-25).[6] Perhaps He said this because wealthy people tend to place their confidence in their wealth instead of in God. Of course, the poor can become bitter in their desire for prosperity, and that also displaces God.

Myth Number Nine: The value of faith lies in its social results.

Some Christian students are turned off to liberalism and attracted to conservatism because conservatives say nicer things about Christianity. It's true that conservatives are less likely to bash religion, but be careful: You may think a person is praising what we believe because he thinks it's true, but he may be praising it merely because he thinks it's useful. Former President Dwight D. Eisenhower is said to have remarked, "Our government has no sense unless it is founded on a deeply religious faith, *and I don't care what it is.*" Recently a book was published with the title *Why America Needs Religion.* Sounds Christian, right? Guess again. The author was an atheist!

When people say America "needs religion," what they usually mean is that religious people commit fewer crimes, have more stable marriages, and have fewer illegitimate children than nonreligious people. In other words, America "needs religion" because it needs these good results. I don't deny that these results are good, but even so, there are three problems with this way of thinking.

First, if results are the only things that matter, then a false religion that has the desired results is just as good as a true one. Not only that, but if results are the only things that matter, then if you could find a way to produce these results without religion you wouldn't need religion after all. Most important of all, if results are the only things that matter, you aren't really worshiping God—you're worshiping results.

THE TRUE COUNTRY

I said this chapter would move swiftly, so this time I'll spare you the summary. Instead let's go a little further. What is politics, anyway? Politics is the art of living as fellow citizens. But what are fellow citizens? Fellow citizens are people who owe loyalty to the same country. Then where is our citizenship—what is our country?

Different readers will give different replies. Most will say "the United States." Some may say "England," "Canada," or another country name. Those answers are perfectly all right, but if you belong to Christ you can give a deeper one. The country you named may be your country by birth, but you have another country by adoption. The apostle Paul named it in his letter to the Philippians 3:20 when he said, "Our citizenship is in heaven." That's the true country of every Christian. On earth, you're only a visitor, and someday you're going home.

Am I saying that you shouldn't respect the earthly government or law? Not at all; in fact, the Bible requires us to respect them. Just remember that you're also under a higher government, God's, and a higher Law, His command. Then am I saying that just because your true citizenship is in heaven, you shouldn't get involved in earthly causes? No, that would be like saying that just because your citizenship is in heaven, you shouldn't eat earthly food or breathe earthly air. Just remember you have a higher cause as well—to represent the King. Better than a constitution, you have a gospel. Better than a president, you have a Savior. Better than a flag, you have a cross.

CONFUSED?

Eight in ten Americans call themselves Christians, but only three in ten know why Easter is celebrated.

Four in ten Americans say the Bible is the "totally accurate" Word of God, but only three in ten say it is the ultimate authority in matters of truth.

Four in five Americans say "there are clear guidelines about what's good and evil that apply to everyone regardless of the situation," but more than three in five say "there are few absolutes."

—THOMAS C. REEVES, "NOT SO CHRISTIAN AMERICA"[7]

HOW TO COPE

Chapter 8

COPING IN CAMPUS SOCIAL LIFE

"HOW TO"

Walk into any bookstore. You'll find books about how to be popular, books about how to catch a mate, books about how to get rich, books about how to influence other people, and books about how to win elections. A few months ago I even saw a book called *How to Be a Lesbian.*

These books are jam-packed with rules. There are more rules in them than you'd ever find in the Bible. But unlike the Bible's rules, they aren't for helping you stay in holy love with God—they're for helping you stay in greedy love with yourself. For Christians, social life is how the love that the triune God gives to you breaks out of you again into love for other people; it's the way you imitate His love in daily life. But *self*-love *can't* break out into love for other people. If you follow that kind of love, social life turns into a hall of mirrors in which we ought to be looking at other people but can see only ourselves.

Let me show you what I mean. The following quotations come from one of the advice books I'm talking about, a New Age book which lays down a thousand rules while pretending that it doesn't give any rules at all.[1]

"Blessed are the Self-centered, for they shall know God."

"Let each person in relationship worry not about the other, but only, only, only about Self."

"For centuries you have been taught that love-sponsored action arises out of the choice to be, do, and have whatever produces the highest good for another. Yet I tell you this: the highest good is that which produces the highest good for *you*."

"Remember, your job on the planet is not to see how long you can stay in relationship, it's to decide, and experience, Who You Really Are."

"Practice saying ten times each day: I LOVE SEX. Practice saying *this* ten times: I LOVE MONEY. Now, you want a really tough one? Try saying *this* ten times: I LOVE *ME!*"

The author even tries to present selfishness as a "holy cause"! Maybe you're thinking, "Come on, no one is taken in by views like that." If so, you've got another think coming. The book I'm quoting has been on *The New York Times* Bestseller List for more than a year, and people don't usually shell out hard cash to buy books they aren't taken in by. Quite a few other best-sellers give much the same advice. Self-love is what worldly social life is all about, and if it hasn't hit you in the face already, it will when you get to college. From every direction the Enemy will be whispering, "Think this way too; yes, think this way too. This way is happiness. This way is joy. This way is knowing Who You Really Are." Actually that way is pain, loneliness, and never really knowing anyone else. The Christian view of social life is a *sacrificial* view. We sacrifice ourselves for others as Christ sacrificed Himself for us. And strangely, His way of forgetting the self is the only way to find the self.

So let's talk about campus social life from a different point of view. Let's talk about it from a biblical point of view—from a godly point of view. Yes, I'll give you some advice—and yes, if you insist you can call it "rules." But remember that we don't follow God because we want to stay in love with rules; we follow certain rules because we want to stay in love with God—Wonderful Counselor, Everlasting Father, Prince of Peace.

Friends and Acquaintances

What is friendship? In the broadest sense, friendship is a personal relationship based on trust between people who know each other well and do some kind of good for each other.

That definition covers a lot of territory. The friendship Abraham enjoyed with God was different from the one David enjoyed with Jonathan. The friendship a husband enjoys with his wife is different from the one a sales representative enjoys with a client. Children enjoy a different kind of friendship with their parents than they do with companions their own age. Students enjoy a different kind of friendship with a trusted teacher than they do with each other. These relationships can vary according to whether the friends are close or distant, whether they are equal or unequal, or whether they are of the same sex or opposite sexes. Finally, they can have different foundations: They can be based on kinship, fun, or mere familiarity. They can be grounded on sharing a task, sharing a cause, or sharing a whole life. Each kind of friendship has its own customs, its own laws, its own expectations.

After the first year, college students don't ask many questions about how to make friends; almost everyone knows something about that. With a few exceptions, the loneliest students aren't lonely because they don't know how to say, "Hi, I'm Eric," but for other reasons. They might be lonely because they make the wrong friends, because they look for them in the wrong places, because they expect others to make friends with *them,* or even because they base their lives on empty philosophies.

A big problem for many students—and one they ask many questions about—is problems and tensions with the friends they already have. Tension may arise because one friend desires a close relationship, while the other wants to keep his distance. Even tougher is when one friend desires a different *kind* of friendship than the other. That's especially common when the friends are of the opposite sex: For example, Linda sees Mike as a "friend who happens to be a boy," but Mike sees Linda as a "girlfriend." When friends can't agree about what kind of friendship to have, sometimes they can't maintain a friendship at all. They have to break up.

Friendships both form and break up more readily when you're young than at any other time in your life, so let's talk about breakups a bit longer. We've looked at two reasons friends break up; what are some others? One reason is that the friends change so much that they no longer have anything in common; big changes are typical when people go to college. You can see how a big change for the worse can bring an end to friendship; you may have to drop Sally because she becomes involved in drugs. But a big change for the better can have the same result: Sally may drop you because you won't do drugs with her anymore.

Still another reason friendships end is that although neither you nor your friend has changed, as you get to know him better you discover that he isn't the person you thought he was. At first, you thought Mark was an honest guy—but then he ran up your telephone bill with long-distance calls and paid you with a hot check. It can also happen that differences that didn't seem important to either friend at the

The Pain of Disloyalty

If an enemy were insulting me,
I could endure it;
if a foe were raising himself against me,
I could hide from him.
But it is you, a man like myself,
my companion, my close friend,
with whom I once enjoyed sweet fellowship
as we walked with the throng at the house of God.
—DAVID, PSALM 55:12-14

beginning of a relationship start grating on at least one of them later. At first, Sheila didn't mind that you wouldn't cut church to do things with her, but now she does; at first, you didn't mind that she made cracks about your church friends, but now you do.

With patience and honesty, sometimes differences like this can be worked out, but sometimes they can't. In general, they are much easier to work out among friends who are also both friends with Christ, because then they have the support of the Holy Spirit and of other believers. In a letter to the young church at Philippi, not only does Paul beg the two friends Euodia and Syntyche to get along, but he asks the person reading the letter to help them make up because they have been such faithful partners in the gospel (Philippians 4:2-3).

Another big reason you might break up is that you realize your friend isn't good for you. This is especially likely if he is not a Christian—a problem we discussed from a different perspective in chapter 4. Maybe you'd hoped you'd have a good influence on Kim, but instead you discover that she's having a bad influence on you. Your language is getting coarser, your jokes are getting cruder, your imagination is becoming soiled. You've been doing things that make you uncomfortable. More and more often you're surprised at yourself. At the beginning of the friendship, you hadn't recognized its danger, maybe because you had a higher opinion of your virtue than it deserved. Eventually, you discover not only that you can be tempted, but that you have been tempted; not only that you have been tempted, but that in a hundred little ways you've been giving in. Finally you realize that the only way to stop giving in is to get out.

You can minimize the risk that friendships will die by choosing your friends wisely and looking for them in the right places, like a Christian fellowship group. But you can't reduce the risk to zero. Sometimes a relationship must be allowed to end.

Breaking up confuses many young Christians, because Christian social life is based on love—and isn't love supposed to be forever?

Well, that depends on what you mean by love. Our language calls many things "love," but not all of them are the kind of love the Bible talks about. The only forever-loves I know of are God's love for His people, the love of His people for Him, and their brotherly love for each other. Certain other loves are less than forever but still lifelong, like the union of a Christian man and

Seven Qualities of a True Friendship

1. **You appreciate each other.**
2. **You're loyal to each other.**
3. **You're honest with each other.**
4. **Your relationship is a two-way street.**
5. **You have well-founded trust in each other.**
6. **Neither of you asks the other to do wrong for him.**
7. **Because of the friendship, each of you is a better and more virtuous person.**

woman in marriage: They don't promise to be husband and wife for eternity, but only until they are parted by death. But most relationships aren't like that. In most relationships, it's okay to break up. Pals don't have to find each other fun until death. Business partners don't have to enjoy doing business until death. And you don't have to like the same roommates until death. It isn't a sin to stop *liking*.

No Hard Feelings

Mark deserted Paul and Barnabas during a missionary journey. Barnabas, Mark's uncle, later suggested taking Mark along on another journey, but Paul, viewing Mark as untrustworthy, refused. The disagreement was so serious that Paul and Barnabas parted company too. Yet Paul didn't hold a grudge, for in a later letter he spoke highly of Barnabas. Once Mark had mended his ways, Paul even asked Timothy to send Mark to him to share his work.

For these less-than-lifelong kinds of bonds, the bottom line is that you can stop having that special friend-love for a person, but you have to go on having neighbor-love. Even if the relationship ends, you have to be honest, fair, and kind; you have to continue desiring good for your former friend; and you have to keep from seeking revenge or spreading gossip.

Yes, even if he acts like a rat! Yes, even if he spreads gossip about you! While you're at it, remember that by God's standards, you're pretty ratty too. We all are. That's why we need the Savior.

DATING AND MARRIAGE

Here's where my student readers will split. Some of you will be relieved because I give plain answers to questions that many books refuse to touch. But some of you will be mad because you won't like the answers I give.

The four questions young Christians ask most often about dating are: "Who can I date?"; "Who can I marry?"; "What can I do?"; and "How far can I go?" Let's look at each one in turn.

The answer to the "Who can I date?" question has two parts: (1) You can date anyone it would be okay to marry; and (2) You can't date anyone it wouldn't be okay to marry. Why these rules? Because dating is *about* marriage. It's not a search for fun or a search for sex. It's a search for a suitable marriage partner. Marriage is the state men and women were designed for, not dating. In some societies there's no dating at all, and guess what: As long as the spouses are suitable and the marriages are faithful, God doesn't mind. David and Abigail came together on their own, but Isaac and Rebekah were brought together by their families. Although each marriage came about in a different way, both were pleasing to God.

The answer to the "Who can I marry?" question has three parts: (1) You have to marry a Christian; (2) You have to marry a person who will make a good spouse; and (3) You have to marry a person who will make a good parent.

I already know what you're asking about the first part: Can't you make a good marriage with someone who doesn't follow Christ? Nope. Not what God calls a good marriage. "Do not be yoked together with unbelievers," says Paul in the Bible. "For what do righteousness and wickedness have in common?" (2 Corinthians 6:14). These words may shock you. Are we so righteous? Is everyone else so much more wicked than we are? Doesn't Paul say elsewhere that *all* have sinned and fall short of the glory of God? Yes, of course he does (Romans 3:23). Then when Paul says this, has he changed his mind? Not at all. He doesn't mean that *you're* righteous and the unbeliever is wicked; he means that you've grabbed onto the righteousness of *Christ* and the unbeliever hasn't. Christ offers Himself as a sin offering for the unbeliever too, but the unbeliever refuses to accept Him. Therefore, in the one thing that matters most of all, the believer and the unbeliever are tragically divided. No marriage can paper over that division! It will always be like a canyon between them. The more the believing spouse grows in the love of Christ, the wider and deeper the canyon will grow. And don't start thinking that you can marry someone now and convert him later. How can you count on that, when the marriage itself began in your disobedience to God?

Part two of the "Who can I marry?" question is that you have to marry a person who will make a

The Six Strangest Ways to Get a Wife
Please note that the Bible doesn't *Endorse* them—it merely *Records* them!

1. **Find a man with seven daughters and impress him by watering his flock. (Exodus 2:16-21—Moses and Zipporah)**
2. **Have God create a wife for you while you sleep. Note: This will cost you a rib. (Genesis 2:19-24—Adam and Eve)**
3. **Agree to work seven years for a woman's hand in marriage. Get tricked into marrying the wrong woman, then work another seven years for the one you wanted to marry in the first place. (Genesis 29:15-30—Jacob, Leah, and Rachel)**
4. **Go to a party and hide. When the women come out to dance, grab one and carry her off to be your wife. (Judges 21:19-25 —the Benjamites)**
5. **Become the emperor of a huge domain and hold a beauty contest. (Esther 2:2-4—Xerxes, also known as Ahasuerus, and Esther)**
6. **When you see someone you like, go home and tell your parents, "I have seen a woman; now get her for me as my wife." If your parents question your decision, just say, "Get her for me. She's the right one for me." (Judges 14:1-3—Samson and the Philistine woman)[2]**

good spouse. Sounds easy, but the hard part is to follow God's idea of what a good spouse is, not your own. Paul compares the relationship between husbands and wives to the relationship between Christ and the church (Ephesians 5:22-33). Christ gave Himself for the church, and the church follows Christ as her head; in the same way the husband must give himself for his wife, and the wife must follow her husband as her head. That comparison was shocking when Paul first wrote it because it went against the male-supremacist idea that the wife is just a servant. But it's just as shocking today because it goes against the feminist idea that no one is in authority! If you're a woman, ask yourself this question: Is the man you have in mind capable of giving himself for you—and is he someone you can follow as your head? If you're a man, ask yourself this one: Will the woman you have in mind be capable of accepting your head-ship—and is she someone you can give yourself for?

Part three of the "Who can I marry?" question is that you have to marry someone who will make a good parent. Many young Christians get hung up on this point. They say, "But what if we plan to *never* have children?" Sorry, unless you're biologically incapable, *never* is not an option. God commands spouses to be fruitful and multiply. It's one of the purposes of marriage, one of the ways that it glorifies Him. So if you're a man, you need to be looking for a woman who would make a good mother, and if you're a woman, you need to be looking for a man who would make a good father.

The answer to the "What can I do?" question has two parts: (1) You can do anything on a date that's pure and pleasing to God; and (2) You must be realistic about temptations.

I'm going to take a chance by assuming I don't need to say much about the first part. (Do you *really* think that R-rated movie is pure and pleasing to God?) The second part is where we need to talk, because it's exactly when we're being tempted that we find it hardest to be realistic about what's happening. Let me give you an example. According to research, the more hours a man and woman spend alone together, *even if they begin with a firm intention of chastity,* the further they tend to go and more likely they are to lose control completely. Hearing this, most Christian young people have the good sense to see that couples who really want to remain chaste need to limit their time alone. That's realism. Unfortunately, the more time they've been spending alone, the less obvious such realism will be to them. The solution is that they need to set their limits firmly at the *beginning* of their relationship, while their heads are still clear and realism is easier to achieve.

Finally, the answer to the "How far can I go?" question has three parts: (1) You can't have sexual intercourse; (2) You can't do anything resembling sexual intercourse; and (3) You can't do anything that gets your motor running for sexual intercourse.

I've already written a whole chapter about part one. The point of part two is to answer questions like "Does oral sex count as sex?" "Does full-body grinding with clothes on count as sex?" and "Does it count as sex if we only use our hands?" Come on, don't kid yourself; you know the answers. Pretending you aren't having sex just because there's no vaginal penetration is like pretending you're not naked because your eyes are closed.

Now about part three. You know what I mean by getting your motor running, don't you? I mean doing things that sexually arouse you. Listen, God invented sexual arousal. But for what purpose? *To prepare your bodies for sex.* Leading to sex is what sexual arousal is *for.* Don't say, "We'll do things that sexually arouse us, but we won't let them lead to sex." That is like turning on powerful rocket motors but saying, "Don't lift off." The solution? Avoid the things that arouse you! If sex is only for marriage, sexual arousal must be too.

A big reason many Christian students find abstinence difficult is that they know the rules but haven't seen the vision. Your goal isn't just to avoid something bad—it's to achieve something beautiful and lovable. God calls it Purity. *Mere* abstinence may be dull, but the pure in heart will see God (Matthew 5:8). Through the centuries many Christians have even called purity thrilling—like clear mountain water that sparkles in the sun. Don't knock it until you've tried it.

Clubs and Activities

One of the best things about college is that there are so many fun, interesting, and worthwhile groups and activities to join. There are jazz bands, sports leagues, and acting troupes. There are singing societies, service fraternities, and debating teams. There are religious fellowships, political parties, and associations for particular professions. On my own campus alone there are more than six hundred student groups, with new ones forming every week. Every wall, tree trunk, and bulletin board is covered with their posters. One day recently, I heard a student singing group I'd never heard of perform for free in the open-air dining area just outside the student union—great music, no instruments, perfect harmony. College is like that.

Many young Christians take advantage of these opportunities, and that's good. Naturally some groups and activities should be avoided. The guidelines here are simple: Avoid any club or pastime that tends to corrupt you, weaken your faith, or lead you into unnecessary temptations. For example, some fraternities seem to exist for sex and some sororities seem to exist for getting drunk. But there are plenty of good clubs and activities left. You're really missing something if you aren't involved in any student organizations.

The most surprising thing is that not all Christian students are involved in worship and Christian fellowship. Gathering with other believers to glorify God, to build each other up in Christ, and to practice acts of mercy toward people in need isn't just one of the choices on the menu. "Should I join chess club or should I join a Christian fellowship instead?" Fellowship is necessary to your relationship with Christ. It's also the best place to form rewarding friendships and find a person suitable to marry. As the Bible says, "Let us consider how we may spur one another on toward love and good deeds. Let us not give up meeting together, as some are in the habit of doing, but let us encourage one another" (Hebrews 10:24-25). We'll talk more about campus religious life in the next chapter, so we'll leave the subject for now.

REMINDERS

We've been all over the map, so let's summarize what we've been saying in this chapter.

Christian life is about being in love with God, and Christian social life is about letting that love break out into your relationships with other people. Friendship is a wonderful opportunity to share His love, but friendships do break up sometimes, even among Christians. If this happens, you can set aside that special friend-love, but you have to go on treating your former friend with neighbor-love.

Dating friendships are unique in that their purpose is to find someone suitable for marriage. This makes things like who we date and how we date much more important than they seem to nonChristian people. For example, because marrying nonbelievers is off-limits, dating them is off-limits too.

Finally, feel free to take advantage of the rich opportunities college offers to join interesting groups and activities. Just remember to avoid any venture that makes you worse or drags you down, and be sure to include a group with whom you can join in Christian worship, fellowship, and acts of mercy.

Chapter 9

Coping in Campus Religious Life

No Such Thing

One day a graduate student visited to tell me that he'd been doing something he'd never done before: He'd been thinking about God, and he needed to talk with someone. He asked, "Do you think I'm crazy?"

I assured him that he wasn't, so he told me his story. He said he'd been reading and reading all his ultramodern books. None of the writers said anything about God, and it had finally occurred to him that "they're building their theories on nothing."

Over time he became a believer in Christ, but for some reason he refused to gather for worship or fellowship with other believers. To fellow students who wanted to encourage him in his newfound relationship with God, he merely said, "I don't need church to be a Christian. I can be a Christian by myself."

But it wasn't true. As the months went by, his friends saw him drift further and further from Christ, and the adventure of faith seemed to fizzle.

A solitary Christian? No such thing.

College may be a turning point in your walk with God—a time when your relationship with Christ either deepens or weakens. For most young Christians, what makes the greatest difference in which way they go is whether they stay in constant close fellowship with their brothers and sisters in the faith.

The Importance of Personal Worship

On my bed I remember you;
I think of you through the watches of the night.
Because you are my help,
I sing in the shadow of your wings.
My soul clings to you;
your right hand upholds me.

—Psalm 63:6-7

WHAT GOES ON?

What goes on in Christian fellowship? Many things, so let's take them one at a time.

The first is *worship*. Worship is expressing to God our love and praise. Sometimes we worship by making a joyful noise, sometimes by silently adoring. One reason we worship is that it's natural. When you see something wonderful you want to wonder, when you're in love you want to speak of love, and when you're with God you want to worship.

Another reason is that it's fitting. If we can't praise what's worthy of praise then there's something wrong, and God is more worthy than anything we can imagine.

The last reason to worship is that God commands it. He knows our needs; if He says we need to worship, we do.

The second aspect of fellowship is *group prayer*. Much nonsense has been written and said about prayer; one writer says that having a quiet cup of coffee and looking out the window is prayer. That might be nice, but it isn't prayer. Prayer is worshipful, personal conversation with the living God, including praising Him, giving thanks, confessing sin, presenting to Him our requests for ourselves and others, and listening to Him. Everyone needs quiet daily private prayer with God, but everybody needs regular group prayer with God too. Why? Because we're not just lone individuals; God has made us members of the body of Christ. More about that later in the chapter.

The third is *learning*. The Psalms say to God, "How can a young man keep his way pure? By living according to your word" (Psalm 119:9). Another passage tells what will happen if you do this: "For wisdom will enter your heart, and knowledge will be pleasant to your soul. Discretion will protect you, and understanding will guard you" (Proverbs 2:10-11). With words like these the Bible urges us to learn God's wisdom, so we gather together to study it.

The fourth is *encouragement and support*. Christian fellowship is like a family where we can bear the burdens of others and urge each other on. Those who have more experience in the faith model Christ to those who have less. Because we know each other well, we can also hold each other accountable, ringing alarm bells about sin and helping each other confess to God and get back on our feet.

The Importance of Corporate Worship

Do not get drunk on wine, which leads to debauchery. Instead, be filled with the Spirit. Speak to one another with psalms, hymns and spiritual songs. Sing and make music in your heart to the Lord, always giving thanks to God the Father for everything, in the name of our Lord Jesus Christ.
—EPHESIANS 5:18-20

The last is *outreach.* Outreach has two meanings: evangelism and mercy. Evangelism is telling outsiders the good news of Jesus Christ in words; mercy is displaying it to them in deeds. Both are commanded by God, and both are more effective when Christians cooperate. An example of cooperative evangelism might be sponsoring a debate between a Christian and an atheist and inviting our nonbelieving friends to attend. An example of cooperative mercy might be organizing visits to the sick and elderly in nursing homes. We can invite our nonbelieving friends along on mercy projects too. By encouraging them to give of themselves, we bring them closer to opening their hearts to Christ.

One more thing. I focus in this chapter on *student* Christian groups. They're important—in my view, crucial—but I don't want to give the impression that if you're in a student Christian group you're having all the Christian fellowship you need. You also need to be in a "real" church. I can hear you saying, "But I'd rather just be with people like me!" But that's just it: We'd *all* like to be with people like ourselves. But that's a selfish impulse that Christ wants to help us overcome. A student Christian group is like a club, but a church is more like a village. It has old and young, knowledgeable and naive, easy to get along with and hard to get along with. Learning to love all those people is just the kind of practice you need! So find a good student fellowship, but find a good church too. You'll find that most of the pointers in this chapter about finding good student fellowships also apply to finding good churches.

WHAT TO LOOK FOR

You won't find perfection until you get to heaven. However, some campus Christian fellowships are more in tune with Jesus than others, so here's a short checklist of things to look for when you arrive on campus.

Look for a fellowship that openly acknowledges Jesus Christ as Lord and Savior. The members should be clear about their loyalty. Jesus said, "Whoever acknowledges me before men, I will also acknowledge him before my Father in heaven. But whoever disowns me before men, I will disown him before my Father in heaven" (Matthew 10:32-33).

Look for a fellowship that accepts the Bible as the true and authoritative Word of God to man. What the Bible teaches, the

Finding Christian Friends

Don't let dorm life fool you. It's hard, and true friends are hard to come by....
I found true and genuine Christians—you just had to look a little harder.

—Anonymous college student

members should believe. What the Bible commands, the members should be trying to do.

Look for a fellowship that understands that we are made right with God by faith in Christ, not by our own good deeds. We can't earn our way into heaven; only Christ's own righteousness was pure enough. We're reconciled with God not *by* doing good, but *in order* to do good.

Look for a fellowship that holds members to high and clear standards of moral conduct. Of course we all sin. But we should be helping each other not to sin. Certainly we should forgive those who repent of their wrongdoing, but we shouldn't act as though wrongdoing doesn't matter. As God told the people of Israel, "Be holy because I, the LORD your God, am holy" (Leviticus 19:2).

Look for a fellowship whose members are not quarrelers or backbiters, but have sacrificial love for each other. I can't beat Jesus' own words: "A new command I give you: Love one another. As I have loved you, so you must love one another. By this all men will know that you are my disciples, if you love one another" (John 13:34-35).

Look for a fellowship with good balance. The life of the group should be evenly balanced among worship, prayer, learning, encouragement and support, and outreach. It should work on both strengthening old members and drawing in new ones. There should be mutual respect and good communication between the leadership and the rest of the group.

Finally, look for a group that will challenge you to grow in Christian maturity. Be part of a group whose members are advancing, with the help of the Holy Spirit, toward greater and greater love of Christ, trust in Christ, and obedience to Christ.

WHAT TO AVOID

Not all campus Christian fellowships live up to the name of Christ. Sometimes the label "Christian" is even used by groups that have nothing to do with the historic Christian faith. For both of these reasons, you need to be careful in choosing your own fellowship. Here's a checklist of things to avoid.

Avoid groups that reject or twist the Bible. Rejecting the Bible means denying its truth or its authority, by saying it was "just a product of its times," for example. Twisting it means using tortured interpretations to try to escape what it really says, such as saying the "new birth" is about reincarnation rather than becoming a new person in Christ.

Avoid groups that demean or dilute the Bible. Demeaning the Bible means not taking it seriously, by picking and choosing which parts to follow, for example. Diluting it means treating it as merely one of many revelations, such as setting up the *Urantia Book* or the *Book of Mormon* as another sacred text alongside it.

Avoid groups that treat exotic or emotional experiences as the main feature of Christian life. God promises every Christian the gift of His Holy Spirit, but He does not promise every Christian that he will have special "spiritual" experiences like prophetic dreams or special "spiritual" emotions like weeping with joy. In fact, the Bible teaches that we should "test everything" to make sure it really comes from God (1 Thessalonians 5:21).

Avoid groups that idolize their human leaders. Leadership is necessary, but Christian leaders are to lead by being servants (John 13:1-17). A healthy Christian fellowship is focused on the triune God, not on the personalities of the people in charge.

Avoid groups that try to cut you off from your family. If you become a Christian but your family is opposed, it's true that you can expect tension. However, a healthy Christian fellowship will encourage you to model the love and patience of Christ to your family, not to break off your relationships with family members.

Avoid groups that try to mix Christianity with other religions. Some religions teach that there are many roads to God and that Jesus is only one of them. Jesus Himself taught the opposite, saying, "I am the way and the truth and the life. No one comes to the Father except through me" (John 14:6).

Scripture Twisters

James W. Sire, *Scripture Twisting: Twenty Ways the Cults Misread the Bible*.[1]

Norman L. Geisler and Ron Rhodes, *When Cultists Ask: A Popular Handbook on Cultic Misinterpretations*.[2]

Avoid groups that try to mix Christianity with occultic practices. Examples of occultic practices are trying to communicate with spirits other than God, trying to induce abnormal mental states, and trying to foretell the future. The Bible calls such practices "sorcery" and warns against them in the strongest possible terms (Galatians 5:19-21).

WHAT NOT TO WORRY ABOUT

Sometimes Christian students pass by perfectly good fellowships for superficial reasons. Following are examples of things not to worry about—things that may seem to matter, but really don't.

Don't worry just because it takes a while to fit in. You won't feel comfortable on your first or second visit. Give yourself some time. Don't wait until you feel completely comfortable before you participate;

the higher your level of participation, the more quickly you'll feel comfortable.

Don't worry just because you don't feel fond of every single member. The members of a Christian fellowship should all have brotherly love for each other, but even among Christians it's inevitable that you'll like some people more and others less. Liking isn't the same as loving anyway. Liking is a feeling of affection for another person, but Christian love is a commitment to the other person's true good. You should *try* to like because it makes love easier—but you don't have to "click" with everyone.

Don't worry just because the group does things a little differently from the way you like. Maybe the group doesn't sing your favorite Christian songs, or maybe it worships in a slightly different style than the one you're used to. You can probably get used to little differences like that. In fact, your preferences about them may even change. Much more important is whether the life of the group is based on the Word of God and the solid rock of Christ.

Don't worry just because not everyone in the group has the same level of commitment and understanding. Some people may be firm in faith and others shaky; some may know much about the Bible and others little. That's okay. The important thing is that the people in leadership have strong faith and understanding, and that throughout the group the stronger members help the weaker ones along.

Don't worry if other people don't think the group is cool. We Christians are the nonconformists of today. Naturally, the conformists don't think we're cool. The more you think about the things that *are* considered cool, the harder it is to see any attraction in them. Think about it: What's so great about empty sex? What's so great about getting drunk? What's so great about frying your brain on dope?

Here is a final thought about things that don't matter. On and around most campuses there are dozens of Christian fellowships—all kinds of them. *If with so many choices you still can't find one you're willing to join, you need to start asking whether the problem isn't them, but you.* You might not be seriously looking. Why wouldn't you seriously look? There are a thousand reasons not to. For example, maybe you've always thought of yourself as a Christian, but you've never truly given yourself to Christ. Maybe you've done something wrong, it bothers your conscience, and you're looking for an excuse to lose your faith so you don't have to think about it. Maybe you're spiritually arrogant, or maybe you're just plain lazy.

Am I making you mad? If so, that's a strong sign that you need to pray about the matter. Ask God to hold up a mirror so you can look into yourself. Repent if you need to. Then ask Him to help you find the Christians that He wants you to be with.

THE BODY OF CHRIST

The Bible says two wonderful things about Christian fellowship. The first is about the church, and the second is about you as a member of the church.

You see, the church is not a building. It's not even just a group of people. It's much more than that. The church—all those who are united in Christ—is Christ's body. Christ is the head. And you, as a member, are a part of His body (1 Corinthians 12:12-27).

What is a body? It's the physical way someone acts in the world. His head leads and his body does as the head directs. He grips with his hands, he stands with his feet, he walks with strong movements of his legs, he speaks with his mouth, he listens with his ears.

When the Bible says the church is the body of Christ, it's telling you that during the present age, those who are united in Christ are the physical means by which *He* acts in the world. They are *His* way of doing things, *His* way of making His will come to pass. The hands, the feet, the legs, and all the other parts—all of them depend on each other and all of them have tasks for the good of the whole. You do too.

What does Christ want to do in the world? He told His disciples that He wants to make it His own. He instructed them to go and make disciples of all nations. Does that include today? Of course it does. Does it include colleges and universities? Of course it does. Are these colleges and universities pagan? By and large, yes. But so what! A pagan is just someone who isn't a Christian yet. Christ is using His body to reach out to our pagan colleges and universities and call them back to Himself. He wants you to be part of the project. If you are a limb, then be a limb! Turn in the joint where you're placed! There's no greater privilege on earth. Find your job in the body of Christ, and get going.

Some Good Campus Christian Organizations

Campus Crusade for Christ
http://www.ccci.org/

InterVarsity Christian Fellowship
http://www.gospelcom.net/iv/

Navigators Collegiates
http://www.gospelcom.net/navs/collegiate/

International Students (ISI)
http://www.isionline.org/

Chapter 10

COPING IN THE CLASSROOM

SHAFTS OF LIGHT

I said in the opening chapter that there's a point of no return in the intellectual denial of God, and when Jesus Christ got to me I was almost there. To keep from facing God, I had pulled one component after another from my mind, and I had nearly got to the motherboard. The few years after my conversion were like being in a dark attic where I'd been for a long time, but where shutter after shutter was thrown back so that great shafts of light streamed in to illuminate the dusty corners. I recovered whole memories, whole feelings, whole ways of understanding the world that I'd blocked out so that I wouldn't see Him.

My story will be different from yours, but it illustrates a general truth. If I asked all my Christian students, "What happens when you become a Christian?" most would probably give me answers like these: "Your sins are forgiven." "You develop a personal relationship with Jesus Christ." "You clean up your act." "You become part of the church." "God starts changing you from within." "You begin to care more about other people." All of those answers are true, but there's another one that Christian students sometimes overlook. When you submit yourself to Christ, *your mind is renewed.*

It isn't just your emotions, your behavior, and your relationships with God and other people that change— if you cooperate with the Holy Spirit, you get a whole new mind! Paul says, "Do not conform any longer to the pattern of this world, but be transformed by the renewing of your mind. Then you will be able to test and approve what God's will is—his good, pleasing, and perfect will" (Romans 12:2).

Let's Dig Up the Dirt on the Author

If you want to read the rest of my story, take a look at http://www.leaderu.com/real/ri9801/budziszewski.html.

DEVELOPING A CHRISTIAN MIND

What does it mean for your mind to be renewed? It means that your thinking has a completely different starting point than it had apart from Christ. The Bible calls this starting point a kind of "fear." "The fear of the LORD is the beginning of wisdom," says Proverbs 9:10, "and knowledge of the Holy One is understanding." Many students don't like that kind of talk; it makes them uncomfortable. So let's take a look at what it really means.

What kind of fear is the fear of the Lord—is it fear that the Lord will do something terrible to you on the day of judgment? No. If you've given yourself to Jesus Christ, *that* kind of fear is gone forever, cast out by the confidence that comes from the love between you and Him (1 John 4:15-18). The debt of your sins has been paid, and He's not going to damn you. But He's still the Holy One, and we tremble to stand in His presence. He won't rest until He has done whatever it takes to make us holy too, and let's be honest—some of the good He intends for us is so far beyond what we can now imagine that we aren't even capable of desiring it yet! Submission to a Lord like that is fearful indeed, but in a wonderful way. We don't fear God because He's bad. We stand in utter awe before Him because He's so good it's scary.

Another thing that's so good it's scary is His Word. Take a look at what Hebrews 4:12 says about it: "For the word of God is living and active. Sharper than any double-edged sword, it penetrates even to dividing soul and spirit, joints and marrow; it judges the thoughts and attitudes of the heart." Can you say that about any other book? Is there another one that pierces right into you, finds you out, and exposes you to yourself? And that's not all. As you study it in fellowship with other Christians, God will be right there beside you, instructing you. Jesus spoke about that at His last meal with His disciples. He promised to send the Holy Spirit to guide His people into "all truth."

If you learn to fear God in the biblical sense, the awe of Him will spread through all your thinking. It will be a fountain of life (Proverbs 14:27). It will make you wise, and it will give you humility (Proverbs 15:33). You will avoid evil not merely out

The Right Kind of Fear and the Right Kind of Fearlessness

The fear of the LORD is the beginning of wisdom, and knowledge of the Holy One is understanding.

—PROVERBS 9:10

"Are not two sparrows sold for a penny? Yet not one of them will fall to the ground apart from the will of your Father. And even the very hairs of your head are all numbered. So don't be afraid; you are worth more than many sparrows."

—MATTHEW 10:29-31

of a sense of duty, but because you love God and you hate what He hates (Proverbs 8:13). In all your ways you'll acknowledge Him, and He will make your paths straight (Proverbs 3:6). You will love Him not only with all your heart, soul, and strength, but also with all your *mind* (Luke 10:27). *That's* what it means for your mind to be renewed.

It may come as a surprise to you that Christ is so interested in your intellect! But of course your teachers are interested in your intellect too, and sometimes that causes a tug of war.

PRACTICING DISCERNMENT

Discernment is a Christian intellectual virtue, like wisdom. A "virtue" is a trait you should have, like love, courage, gentleness, and faithfulness. An "intellectual" virtue is a virtue of the mind, like wisdom. So just what kind of intellectual virtue *is* discernment, then? To answer that question, let's start with something you know already. You know that there are many false things that seem true and many evil things that seem good, right? Well, discernment is what helps you recognize the difference between them. It's what helps you choose the true and avoid the false, choose the good and avoid the evil. It's a mental sense of smell that helps you notice when "something smells fishy." Here are some examples.

Your biology teacher says: "Science shows that the world is aimless, purposeless, and without meaning." *You think:* "Something smells fishy. How could science 'show' a thing like that? Could I point a meaning-meter at the wonder of life and see the needle swing to 'empty'?"

Your physics teacher says: "The material universe is all there is, all there was, and all there ever will be." *You think:* "Something smells fishy. Don't even physicists say that the material universe had a beginning? If it had a beginning, didn't something have to make it begin?"

Your world religions teacher says: "The Bible is patriarchal and sexist because it subordinates women to men." *You think:* "Something smells fishy. I know the Bible calls the husband the head of the wife, but doesn't it also say he should love and give himself up for her the way Christ loved and gave himself up for the church—the ultimate sacrifice?"

Your literature teacher says: "Asking what the author

Clueless

[Man] is the result of a purposeless and natural process that did not have us in mind.

—George Gaylord Simpson, *The Meaning of Evolution*[1]

The fool says in his heart, "There is no God."

—PSALM 14:1

'means' by his story is a mistake. You can never know what anyone really means; all you can know is what his words mean to you." *You think:* "Something smells fishy. If I can't ever know what anyone means, then how can I ever know what my teacher means when he says that?"

In all of these examples discernment warns you that something smells fishy. But it can also encourage you because something smells good. Something might also smell good to you but bad to a nonbeliever. Here's how Paul explains the Christian sense of smell: "But thanks be to God, who . . . through us spreads everywhere the fragrance of the knowledge of him. For we are to God the aroma of Christ among those who are being saved and those who are perishing. To the one we are the smell of death; to the other, the fragrance of life" (2 Corinthians 2:14-16). As you can see, Paul says that how things smell depends on whether you are "being saved" or "perishing"—whether your nose is facing toward Christ or away from Him.

How can you sharpen this mental sense of smell? How can you develop discernment?

First, you need to have a *spirit of obedience* to Jesus Christ. If your spirit is in rebellion, your nose will be in rebellion too.

Second, you need to *study* the Word of God and other Christian literature. We're talking about a mental, not physical, sense of smell. In order to develop it you have to use your mind.

Third, you need to *practice* smelling. Smell everything. Your power of discernment is like a muscle. Use it or lose it.

Fourth, you need to be *accountable* to other believers in a healthy Christian fellowship. If you try to learn to smell by yourself, your mental sense of smell will be eccentric. You'll be like someone who takes a deep whiff of dung and says, "Ah, roses!"

Most importantly, you need to *ask God* for discernment. Scripture gives a vivid sense of how much you should want it by saying you should "call out" and "cry aloud" for it (Proverbs 2:3). When God asked Solomon what he wanted, Solomon asked God for discernment—nothing else. God was so pleased that He gave Solomon not only what he'd requested, but more. Before you go on to the next section, take a break and read the story of his request. You'll find it in 1 Kings 3:5-14.

HOLDING YOUR OWN WITHOUT BEING A JERK

As you acquire discernment, how do you put it to work in the classroom? We've all known people who were on the right side of an issue, but drove people away because of the way they defended it.

Sometimes in the classroom an opportunity arises to share a Christian perspective on the topic under discussion or to stand up for Christian faith when it's under attack. How can you hold up your end of the argument without making Christianity seem obnoxious?

First let me illustrate the *wrong* way to hold up your end of the argument (yes, it's just a bit exaggerated). You're in sociology class, and the professor is just finishing a lecture in favor of relativism. He concludes by saying that no one should claim superiority for his own moral ideas, then asks for questions. As soon as the words are out of his mouth, you stand up, all flushed and angry, face your fellow students, point at the professor, and proclaim, "WOE TO THE WICKED! It shall be ill with him, for what his hands have done shall be done to him! O my people, your leaders mislead you, and confuse the course of your paths!"

Would the professor be ashamed? Would your classmates be convinced? Of course not. The professor would merely raise a quizzical eyebrow and say to the class, "See what I mean?" And the students would think to themselves, "We sure do." Could you blame them?

So let's rewind the tape a few seconds and try again. We're back to the end of the lecture.

Professor:	. . . And so you see how intolerant it is for anyone to claim superiority for his own moral ideas. Any questions?
You:	Do you think intolerance is wrong, sir?
Professor:	Of course. No one should be intolerant. Don't you agree?
You:	Yes, I do. But aren't you claiming superiority for your own moral idea?
Professor:	I don't recall having expressed one. Did I express one?
You:	Yes, sir, I think you did.
Professor:	When?
You:	Just now.
Professor:	What moral idea did I express?
You:	The moral idea that intolerance is wrong.
Professor	Oh, I see. Yes, I guess that is a moral idea. But I didn't claim superiority for it, did I?
You:	Well, sir, I thought you did.
Professor:	You're certainly a persistent young person. Just how did I do that?
You:	By saying that *no one* should be intolerant. Doesn't that imply that your

view that intolerance is bad is superior to the opposing view that intolerance is good?

Professor: Hmmm. Perhaps it does. What's your point?

You: Well, if some moral ideas *are* superior to others, wouldn't that mean relativism is false?

Professor: That's a thought. That's certainly a thought. I'll have to think about that. Next question?

It's All Right to Be Humorous

Teacher: Welcome, students. Since this is the first day of class, I want to lay down some ground rules. First, since no one has the truth, you should be open-minded to the opinions of your fellow students. Has anyone a question? Elizabeth?

Elizabeth: Yes, I do. If nobody has the truth, isn't that a good reason for me *not* to listen to my fellow students? After all, if nobody has the truth, why should I waste my time listening to other people and their opinions? What would be the point? Only if somebody has the truth does it make sense to be open-minded. Don't you agree? . . .

Teacher: This should be an interesting semester.

—Francis J. Beckwith and Gregory Koukl, "A Funny Thing Happened on the Way to the Apocalypse"[2]

Did you notice all the things you did right in *this* conversation? First, you limited yourself to a single point. All you were trying to show was that even your teacher believed in at least one moral truth. Second, you didn't lecture. Your remarks were brief, and most of them were answers to your teacher's questions. Third, you reasoned simply and clearly. Anyone could have followed your line of argument. Fourth, you didn't Bible-bash your teacher. There's a time for quoting Scripture (for example, if the question under discussion is what Jesus said about Himself), but you recognized that this wasn't it. Fifth, you modeled courtesy. You showed respect for your teacher and listened to what he had to say without interrupting. Sixth, you stayed calm. You didn't get flustered, excited, impatient, or angry. Seventh, you recognized that you didn't have to "win." So what if the professor wasn't convinced? So what if he got the last word? So what if he changed the subject? All you had to do was plant a seed.

The same seven guidelines apply when you're responding to comments from your classmates. If you keep all seven in mind, you'll be in good shape.

Dealing with Hostile Teachers

The professor in the previous section disagreed with Christian views, but he tried to be fair. You might run across a bully of a teacher who doesn't even seem to try. How should you respond? Of course it's always good to pray that God will turn your teacher's heart (just don't do it out loud). Another thing you can do is be such a hard worker that even an unfair teacher will find it difficult to complain about you. What else you can do depends on the kind of attack you're dealing with. The three main kinds of attacks are ridicule, partiality in moderating class discussion, and bias in grading.

Case 1: Ridicule. Please remember that it isn't wrong for a teacher to disagree with your opinion! If mere disagreement bothers you, develop a thicker skin. What do I mean by ridicule, then? Things like sneering, name-calling, and intimidation—for example, when a teacher at my own university opened her class by saying, "All of you here are too intelligent to be pro-life, right?"

What can you do about ridicule? In the first place, stay calm; anger gives Satan a foothold. In the second place, challenge the ridicule—but do so calmly, concisely, and politely. "Excuse me, professor. I'm pro-life. You're entitled to correct my facts or my reasoning, but not to insult me before you've even heard them."

If ridicule persists despite your challenge, document it. Write down exactly what was said and when. When you've documented a number of incidents of ridicule and have a number of witnesses who will back you up, then take your complaint to your dean. Almost every college and university disciplines faculty for ridiculing students.

Case 2: Partiality in moderating class discussion. Remember that it isn't unfair for a teacher to take sides! The issue is *how* the teacher takes sides. For example, it's all right if the teacher says he's an atheist, but it's not all right if he calls only on atheists and never on theists, or if he pitches only easy questions to the atheists and only hard ones to the theists.

What can you do about partiality? Don't do anything at all unless it's extreme, and don't complain about it in class, because if you make your professor lose face he'll never listen to you again. Instead, speak with him about the problem in his office—politely and without arguing. If that doesn't help, return to his office another day, take along a classmate who will confirm that what you're saying is true, and speak to him politely again. Some teachers are genuinely surprised to hear that they've shown partiality. Once convinced the complaint is true, they quickly change their ways.

If you've followed these guidelines, yet partiality in class discussion persists, ignore it. Although partiality is frustrating, it's almost impossible to prove, and it's unlikely that it will affect your grade anyway. For these reasons, you're unlikely to achieve anything by complaining to a higher authority. Instead, pray for patience; God loves and honors the desire to imitate His longsuffering.

Case 3: Bias in grading. Remember that it isn't bias for a teacher to give you a lower grade than you think you deserve! Teachers *ought* to be tough. Bias is beyond being tough; it's treating equal quality unequally. For example, suppose a teacher assigns the class a position paper on assisted suicide. Some students write in favor of assisted suicide, others write against it. As the professor is returning the graded papers, he remarks, "By the way, the papers against assisted suicide were of higher quality, but I gave them lower grades because I don't agree with their position."

Bias

Introduction to Public Policy [dealt with] many controversial issues. One young man spoke out in favor of the religious side.... Another student turned around and said, "Why don't you just shut up!" There was nervous laughter, which escalated when the teacher said, "Well, I guess she told you!"

—Anonymous college student

What can you do about bias in grading? First consider how bad it is; the difference between a B+ and a B- is probably not worth fighting for. Second consider whether the bias can be proven; in the example given above you can offer the teacher's own statements as proof, but in most cases proof is more difficult. Only if the bias is both extreme and provable should you then appeal the grade to your teacher privately.

What if you make your case to your teacher, but your teacher refuses to budge? Most colleges and universities do permit students to appeal grades to higher authority, but such appeals are usually treated with skepticism. For good reasons, faculty are granted a lot of discretion, so the burden of proof will be on you. For this reason it's not wise to go over your teacher's head unless your case is very strong.

If injustice is done to you for carrying the banner of Christ, remember the words of Jesus: "Blessed are you when people insult you, persecute you and falsely say all kinds of evil against you because of me. Rejoice and be glad, because great is your reward in heaven, for in the same way they persecuted the prophets who were before you" (Matthew 5:11-12). Let go of your anger and pray for your teacher—not in resentment but in love, not just for your own sake but for his.

FINDING INTELLECTUAL SUPPORTERS

When you get to college, it will help you enormously to find a Christian *mentor*. A mentor is a teacher who shares your Christian faith and is willing to talk with you about how it ties in with your studies. Ideally, your mentor has many years of Christian experience and teaches in the same field you're studying. Are there really Christian professors? More than you may think! How can you find them? The leaders of your church or student Christian fellowship group may be able to refer you to Christian professors. You can also check the campus organizations directory to see if there is a faculty Christian fellowship group on campus. If there is, contact the leader and ask if any of the group's members teach in your field and are available to talk with students about the challenges of faith. You might also see if a Christian study center is located near your campus. At my own university, Christian professors even run an advertisement in the student newspaper once or twice a year, signing their names and inviting students to visit to talk about the claims of Jesus Christ. Ask God to lead you to the right mentor.

While you're praying, you might also ask God to help you find peers who can be an intellectual support circle. Now what do I mean by that? I mean a group of friends of your own age who are dedicated to Christ, face the same intellectual challenges, and encourage each other in the faith by talking about them.

If your church or fellowship group functions as an intellectual support circle, that's great. If not, don't worry about it; every church and fellowship group is stronger in some areas than others. The important thing is that everyone in your intellectual support circle is a Christian, so that you build each other up in faith instead of tearing each other down. Perhaps one member of your intellectual support circle is your roommate, one is from your fellowship group, one is from your church, one is from your softball team, and one shares many classes with you because you're taking the same major.

Your intellectual support circle doesn't have to be a club with regular meetings, although it could be. It's enough that you can all talk together, whether all at once or in twos and threes and fours. In my mind, I hear Frank mentioning to his intellectual support circle that ever since his literature class read *Paradise Lost,* he's been troubled by the puzzle of why there is evil in the world. All of the others respond. Ahmed, who is a good listener, asks questions to draw Frank out. Susan, whose brother died of cancer, mentions that he drew encouragement from Paul's discussion of suffering in Romans 8:18-39, and she and Frank look up the passage and talk about what it says. Farhanna, who reads everything she can get her hands on, suggests the book *The Problem of Pain* by the Christian writer C. S. Lewis and offers to loan it to Frank. Then Frank himself remembers the book of Job in the Old Testament and decides to read it again. Do you see how this works?

An intellectual support circle is a great gift of God that will make a difference for the rest of your life. Just one little thing: You may be tempted to treat your intellectual support circle as a substitute for going to church. Can you see how this might happen? You and the others in your intellectual support circle may start feeling that you're a cut above other Christians and don't need to associate with them—or you may start thinking that your discussions are so spiritual that you don't need to do ordinary Christian things like going to church. It's true that Christians who slip into this kind of thinking escape the mistake of thinking that God isn't interested in their minds, but they fall into the opposite mistake of thinking God is interested *only* in their minds. Love the Lord with all your mind, but love Him with all the rest of you too. Faith should be intelligent, but intelligence doesn't have to be proud!

Who Else Might Be a Mentor

If you can't find a Christian professor in your major, who else might be a Christian mentor? You might choose a graduate teaching assistant in your field, someone not connected with your college in your field, or a professor in a related field. Even if you can't find a Christian academic mentor, you should look for a Christian spiritual mentor. This could be any trustworthy and experienced older Christian—from your local church, from your campus fellowship group, even a parent of a friend. By the way, it's usually wiser to seek a mentor who is the same sex as yourself.

CONCLUSION

Chapter 11

THE MEANING OF YOUR LIFE

FITTING CHRIST INTO YOUR LIFE

In a minute I'm going to say something radical. But not yet.

I'll start slowly, saying what you expect me to say.

You know the drill. I talk about how you've found a place in your life for friendship, for learning, for music, and so forth—then I say, "Don't forget to find a place in your life for Christ."

If you're getting ready for college, I say my piece about how you'll need to be well balanced, spending some of your time in class, some in the library, some in extracurricular activities, and so forth—then I'd say, "Don't forget to spend some of your time with Christ."

If you're already in college, I go into my riff about how you've made a place in your plans for your future major, for your future sweetheart, for your future job, and so forth—then I say, "Don't forget to find a place in your plans for Christ."

Yeah, that's nice.

No, it's not.

Doesn't it sound wrong to you too? You may have seen talk like that in some religious books. I have. Or you may have heard talk like that from some advisor. I have. But doesn't it strike a false note?

What's the false note?

The false note is that it leaves you in charge. It's all about fitting Jesus Christ into *your* life, *your* time, *your* plans. You let Him have His place in them, but you still think they're yours.

There hasn't really been any change. It's as though the building belongs to you, but you let Jesus live in one of the apartments. It's as though the kingdom belongs to you, but you let Jesus have one of the cottages. It's as though the schedule belongs to you, but you let Jesus have one of the appointments.

Maybe you're thinking, "Oh, I get it. I shouldn't give Christ just a little place in my life. I should give Him a big place. Well, I can do that."

No, that's not what I mean. Even if you give Him a big place in your life instead of a little one, it's still your life.

And that's the problem.

Jesus Christ doesn't want a place in your life. He doesn't want you to fit Him into your plans.

Then what does He want?

FITTING YOUR LIFE INTO CHRIST

Christ doesn't want a place in your life; He wants it all. He doesn't want you to fit Him into your plans; He wants to fit you into His. You're called to *belong* to Him. Don't take it from me—check it out in the Bible. Paul says in Romans 1:6: "And you also are among those who are called to belong to Jesus Christ."

A lot of people boggle at this idea. Who does Jesus Christ think He is—God? Yes. That's just it. He is. You're not.

You may be in possession of your life, but you don't have clear title. He's the rightful owner because He paid the price. Where did He pay it? On the cross. How did He pay it? In blood. Now you're called to belong to Him.

Another reason some people boggle at this idea is that it seems to take away their freedom. I'm not going to tell you that freedom isn't important. It is. Jesus Himself talked about it. He said He had come to proclaim "freedom for the prisoners" (Luke 4:18). He said of Himself, "If the Son sets you free, you will be free indeed" (John 8:36). Paul said, "It is for freedom that Christ has set us free" and that we are "called to be free" (Galatians 5:1,13). He said that some day creation itself would be "liberated from its bondage to decay" and "brought into the glorious freedom of the children of God" (Romans 8:21).

But the crucial thing is to understand what kind of freedom this is. It's not something different from

Do You Boggle?
bog-gle   ə
Pronunciation: 'bä-g l
> 1: to start with fright or amazement : be overwhelmed
>   \<the mind boggles at the research needed>
> 2: to hesitate because of doubt, fear, or scruples[1]

The True Meaning of Freedom

Jesus said, "If you hold to my teaching, you are really my disciples. Then you will know the truth, and the truth will set you free....I tell you the truth, everyone who sins is a slave to sin. Now a slave has no permanent place in the family, but a son belongs to it forever. So if the Son sets you free, you will be free indeed."

—JOHN 8:31-32,34-36

For you did not receive a spirit that makes you a slave again to fear, but you received the Spirit of sonship. And by Him we cry, "*Abba,* Father."

—ROMANS 8:15

Now the Lord is the Spirit, and where the Spirit of the Lord is, there is freedom.

—2 CORINTHIANS 3:17

It is for freedom that Christ has set us free. Stand firm, then, and do not let yourselves be burdened again by a yoke of slavery.

—GALATIANS 5:1

belonging to Christ; it *is* belonging to Christ. You see, "a man is a slave to whatever has mastered him" (2 Peter 2:19), and everyone is mastered either by his own sinful desires or by Christ. There aren't any other options. The first way we are free from the control of righteousness, but there is no benefit—only futility and death. The second way we are free from the control of sin, and the benefit is holiness and eternal life (Romans 6:16-23). We choose the second kind of freedom.

"Come on," you say. "*That* can't be freedom, can it? Are you serious? How could that work?" To take your questions one at a time: Number one, yes, it can. Number two, yes, I'm serious. But number three, I don't know how it works! I don't know the spiritual technology! God takes care of that. When He takes over, He really takes over. All I can tell you is that it *does* work and that it's wonderful.

Let's get back to how Christ doesn't want a *place* in your life, but *all* of it, that He doesn't want you to fit Him into your plans but to fit you into His.

Maybe you're thinking, "Oh, I get it. I'm supposed to go into full-time ministry or something."

That's not the point either. In a sense, *every* Christian is a full-time minister, whether he's ordained or not (1 Peter 2:9). God may want you to be ordained, then again He may want you to become a dog catcher. He may want you to be a missionary, then again He may want you to become an accountant. The point is that whatever He wants you to become, He wants you to become wholly His. If you catch dogs, catch them as though they were His dogs. (In fact, they are.) If you balance accounts, balance them as though He owned the business. (In fact, He does.) Give Him your nights and days, your coming and going, your getting up and your lying down. Give Him your friendships, your dates, and when the day comes, your marriage and children. Give Him your past in humility, your present in dedication, and your future in hope and trust.

Now let's see how that plays out.

THE REST OF COLLEGE

Let's take it as a given, then, that God wants to dust you off, clean you up, mold you, teach you, and make you a gleaming mirror of His glory. Let's not ask anymore where God fits in your plan for college. Let's ask where college fits in God's plan for your life.

One of Jesus' stories provides a clue. It's called the Parable of the Talents, and it's about a master who entrusts his servants with the care of his money during a long absence. Upon his return, the master finds that one servant has buried his share to keep it safe, while the other two have invested theirs. The bold ones he praises and rewards with yet greater responsibilities, but the timid one he scolds, fires, and orders thrown out of the premises. He even has his share taken away and given to the other two.

Jesus told this story to teach something about the kingdom of heaven. It's not really about the use of money, but about the use of God's gifts. Money is just a metaphor. We can put the point like this: Just as a tough businessman of this world expects his agents to take risks, not burying his money but using it to earn a return, so God expects us to take risks, not burying our talents but using them to build up the kingdom of heaven.

As you were growing up, people may have encouraged you to use your talents. Sure, but how? Perhaps every now and then someone hinted that you should use them for God. The surprise is finding out that this is the only reason they were given to you in the first place. It's as if they were money and He said, "Expand my business for me." Or as if they were seed and He said, "Raise me up a crop."

You may be thinking, "Why should *I* do all that stuff? Is God lazy or something?" That's not how it is. A better way to view the matter is that He's giving us the amazing privilege of participating in His work. He could do everything by Himself and tell us, "Don't get in the way." He could leave us out. Instead, He makes us partners! If you accept your partnership, one day you'll hear the voice of Christ say, "Well done, good and faithful servant! You have been faithful with a few things; I will put you in charge of many things. Come and share your master's happiness!" (Matthew 25:21,23).

Is there a downside? Not if you use your talents for the kingdom. Of course there's a downside if you don't. In that case, your talents will be taken from you and given to others. Only what is based on

Jesus Christ will survive into heaven (Matthew 25:28-29; 1 Corinthians 3:10-15).

Kind of puts a different spin on college decisions, doesn't it? For that matter, on life decisions!

Some students make their college plans according to what professions will give them the greatest incomes. Some make them according to what seems most fun. Some make them by imitating their friends. And some just drift—from activity to activity, from major to major, from subject to subject. None of these is God's way for you to plan. His way is for you to make your college plans according to how you can best *discover, develop,* and *deploy* your talents.

I just mentioned discovering, developing, and deploying. Let's take each one in turn.

Discovering your talents means finding out what they are. College gives you the chance to try out many things to find out what you do well. And I don't just mean in the classroom. True, Sarah learned that she had writing talent through her English courses, but Wendy learned that she had musical talent by joining the college Glee Club. Nathan learned that he had potential as a counselor through his social work classes, but Sean learned that he would make a good handyman by participating in outreach projects with his campus Christian fellowship.

Developing your talents means practicing to make them sharper and adding knowledge to make

Three Kinds of Spiritual Gifts

Motivational gifts are inborn bents of personality that the Holy Spirit purifies when we follow lives of faith and discipleship. These include the "prophetic" or discerning disposition, the "helping" or serving disposition, the "teaching" or training disposition, the "exhorting" or encouraging disposition, the "giving" or sharing disposition, the "leading" or supervising disposition, and the "merciful" or actively compassionate disposition.

—ROMANS 12:6-8; 1 PETER 4:10-11

Ministry gifts are helps provided by the Holy Spirit to enable those whom he has put in church teaching and leadership roles to fulfill their callings. These include apostolic ministry, prophetic ministry, evangelistic ministry, pastoral ministry, and ordinary teaching ministry.

—EPHESIANS 4:11

Manifestation gifts are edifying displays of the power of the Holy Spirit in the life of the church. Although such gifts really exist, the Bible warns that these can be counterfeited and emphasizes the need to test them. It also cautions against giving them too much emphasis, saying that without love they are worthless. These include healing, prophecy, exceptional discernment, tongues and the interpretation of tongues, and many others.

—ACTS 2:17-18; 1 CORINTHIANS 12:7-11, 13:1-3

them deeper. This too can go on both inside and outside of the classroom. Sarah joined the staff of the school newspaper, Wendy took voice classes from the department of music, and Nathan gained counseling experience as a crisis hotline volunteer. Realizing that most handymen are self-employed, Sean took some architectural drawing and practical business courses, then worked summers as a carpenter's helper.

Deploying your talents means putting them to work to build up God's kingdom. Sarah became a freelancer, writing articles from a Christian perspective and selling them to magazines. Wendy organized a teen choir at her church. Nathan and Sean continued the volunteer work they'd already begun in crisis intervention and community housing rehabilitation.

What happens after you graduate?

THE REST OF YOUR LIFE

Your discovery, development, and deployment of your talents will continue throughout your life. As college draws to an end, discovery and development become less important, and deployment becomes more important.

Now here's a surprise: Your talents aren't the only thing you can use to serve God. In fact, you can put your *whole personality* to work. Why not? Didn't God give it to you? Another way to think of the matter is to consider "talents" as including not only skills like counseling and singing, but also

Nine Biblical Tests for Alleged Spiritual Gifts
The apostle Paul warns, "Test everything" (1 Thessalonians 5:21).

1. *Scripture.* Does the alleged gift follow the Word of God rather than the outlook of the world? (Acts 17:10-11; Romans 12:2-3; 1 John 4:1,4-6)
2. *Lordship.* Does it exalt God, and God alone? Specifically, does it exalt Jesus as the incarnate Christ? (Deuteronomy 13:1-5; 1 Corinthians 12:1-3; 1 John 4:1-3)
3. *Fruits.* Does the person who manifests it have Christian speech and character? Be warned that holy speech is not the same as phony God-talk. (Galatians 5:19-24; James 3:5-12; Matthew 7:21)
4. *Edification.* Does it build up the community of believers? (1 Corinthians 14:12,26 in the context of the chapter)
5. *Orderliness.* Is it disciplined and compatible with good order in worship? (1 Corinthians 14:28,33,39-40 in the context of the chapter)
6. *Confirmation.* Do those who have mature spiritual discernment and oversee the congregation judge it authentic? (1 Corinthians 12:10, 14:29; Ephesians 4:11-16)
7. *Meekness.* Does the person manifesting it willingly submit to such testing? (1 Corinthians 14:36-38)
8. *Purity.* Is it free from moral evil as well as the appearance of moral evil? (Psalm 5:4; Malachi 2:17; 1 Thessalonians 5:21-22; James 1:13; 1 Peter 1:16; 3 John 1:11)
9. *Reliability.* If it involves prophecies, have all of them always come true? (Deuteronomy 18:21-22)

personality traits like insight and a cheerful disposition. After all, they too come from God; they're also given to us for His glory. But they too need to be developed. Let's take a look at some ways you can use your whole personality—your talents, in both the narrow sense and the broad—to glorify God.

In your regular employment. Many people have the idea that the only way to serve God in regular employment is through ordained ministry. Far from it! It's true that some jobs offer greater opportunities than others to speak about the faith—I'm thinking of "talking" jobs like teaching, counseling, and public office. But in one way or another, God can be glorified in any honest job. For example, a Christian accountant can glorify God by setting such a high standard of integrity that he makes people want to know his Lord. A Christian doctor can glorify God by healing both rich and poor, irrespective of ability to pay, showing not only skill but compassion. A Christian lawyer can glorify God by remembering that the source of human justice is divine justice and by refusing to use his knowledge to do wrong.

Typical Ways for Using Your Gifts
1. Mentor someone.
2. Teach Sunday school.
3. Raise godly children.
4. Make sandwiches at the soup kitchen.
5. Keep a peaceful and well-ordered home.
6. Volunteer at the Crisis Pregnancy Center.
7. Select a career appropriate to your talents.

In your volunteer activities. Another common mistake is to think that the only way to serve God in volunteer activities is to do something inside a church building. Not at all! Much of God's work does go on there—teaching Sunday school, singing in choir, preparing the church for worship services. But God also sends a lot of it outside the walls of the church. For example, some people comfort the sick, clothe the poor, and go to see people in prison. One of my friends uses his vacations to help out on Christian medical missions to poor countries. He isn't a trained nurse, doctor, or technician, so he spends a lot of time cleaning bedpans. It isn't glamorous, but he says it's glorious.

In your personal relationships. A third popular error is to think that the only way to serve God in personal relationships is to evangelize your friends. Don't believe it! Needless to say, you should evangelize your friends, but don't forget the silent evangelism of listening when they grieve and offering your arm when they stumble. And what about your family? You glorify God by honoring your parents, giving yourself for the man or woman you marry, and raising up any children God may give you in the knowledge and love of the Lord. We sin, of course, but you glorify God by forgiving others, submitting yourself to others, and bearing others' burdens. God means every Christian family and every Christian friendship to be an outpost of the kingdom of heaven, a signal fire of hope in a world that doesn't see hope very often.

In love. The final mistake people make is to think that giving glory to God is a duty. Not for a minute! What would you think of a father who protected his children merely because he thought he ought to, not from love? Not much. Would you think much of a friend who helped you just because he felt an obligation, not because he cared about your life? Of course not. How about God? Does He spend Himself for *us* because of duty? No. He does it because He loves us. Paul said, "Be imitators of God, therefore, as dearly loved children, and live a life of love, just as Christ loved us and gave himself up for us as a fragrant offering and sacrifice to God" (Ephesians 5:1). This tells us that to imitate God is to copy Christ—to love the way He loves. If I don't love the people whose houses I'm working on, what good is it to spend all my spare time in community housing rehabilitation? I'm just a blind set of fingers or a box rattling with tools. If I don't love God Himself, what good is it to have the gift of music and knock myself out teaching tuneless little children to sing His praise? I'm just a CD player or a multimedia computer. "Whoever does not love does not know God, because God is love" (1 John 4:8).

More Exciting Than I Ever Dreamed

It amazed me that I could have a relationship with God. I talked to Him and, through changes in circumstances, He indicated that He heard me. He led me in career paths that are far more expansive and exciting than I ever dreamed. And I asked Him questions and He guided me to appropriate, helpful answers in the Bible.

These things didn't occur just on one obscure, stormy day. It was a genuine two-way relationship with God that I was enjoying on a consistent basis, and still do. Not because I became a saint, but because Jesus Christ will enter anyone's life who truly wants to know Him and follow Him.

—DRAKE UNIVERSITY STUDENT MARILYN ADAMSON, "WHERE I FOUND REAL PURPOSE."[2]
YOU CAN READ THE REST OF HER TESTIMONY AT
http://www.leaderu.com/everystudent/reallife/reallife2.html.

THE REST OF ETERNITY

Now that we've talked about the rest of college and the rest of your life, let's talk about the rest of eternity. Have you noticed that many people dislike discussing heaven? Are you one of them? I used to be. I thought it was selfish to want to go there. But it's not selfish; we want to go there because God made us that way. Heaven is our True Country—our Home. Do you think it's silly to think much about heaven when there's so much to think about in this life? It's not silly; we'll be there much longer than here. Eighty or ninety years doesn't seem like much next to eternity. Do you think it's naive to hope for heaven because we're merely believing what we want to believe? It's not naive; having come to know God, we've learned that His promises can be trusted. The atheist is the one who believes what he wants to believe, for he wants God and heaven *not* to exist. Do you think it's cheap to serve God in the hope of heaven when we ought to be serving Him for His own sake? It's not cheap; serving God in the hope of heaven *is* serving Him for His own sake because enjoying heaven means enjoying *Him.* If there were danger in hoping for heaven, Christ wouldn't have told us about it.

So it's not foolish to hope for heaven. The foolish thing is hoping for heaven without yielding to Christ because Christ Himself is our hope of heaven. He is the Door.

Let's give way to the hope of heaven. Let's talk about it. Let's picture heaven as the last two chapters of John's Revelation picture it. Take these words as poetic imagery rather than literal description, but remember that reality will be better than the images.

Picture all of nature remade, as fresh as on the day of Creation: a brand-new earth and sky with no pain, no death, and no decay.

Picture a beautiful City poised in the air, coming down out of the sky from God: a City so lovely that it makes you think of a bride, made splendid for her husband on their wedding day.

Picture it throwing off sparks of light like a diamond. Picture the gates. Picture the inside.

Picture the City without need of sun or moon for light because the Lord God and the Lamb of God are its light. Picture it without a temple because the Lord God and the Lamb of God are its temple. In this life we go into church to be with God, but in heaven God will be with us far more perfectly than He is here in church.

Picture a throne. Picture a river of life flowing right down the street from it. Alongside the river, picture trees with leaves of healing. Picture God's people, gazing toward the throne. God has wiped away every tear from their eyes.

This is where I end because the next part is beyond even poetic images. I know how John felt in his last two chapters because I am overcome. It is simply this:

They see His Face. His Name is on their foreheads. And they reign with Him forever.

You can be among them. The decisions you make and the path you take right now in school are determining whether or not you will be called one of God's own. Through college and throughout your life, there will be both times of triumph and times of discouragement. There may be times when discouragement cuts so deep that it seems to call triumph into question. Don't let yourself be confused; put these experiences in eternal perspective. When the angel's horn blows the beginning of forever, *that* will be victory, *that* will be triumph.

They see Him face to face. You can be among them. Follow Christ.

ABOUT THE AUTHOR

J. BUDZISZEWSKI (Boojee-shefski) is a former atheist, former political radical, former shipyard welder, and former lots of other things, including former young and former thin. He earned his Ph.D. at Yale, and since 1981 he's been at the University of Texas in Austin, where he teaches in the departments of Government and Philosophy. He's written a couple of books about natural law, and if you ask him what that is he'll say it's what you "can't not know" about right and wrong. We forgot to tell you that he's been married for twenty-six years to his high school sweetheart, Sandra, a crisis pregnancy center counselor, and has two daughters, one just starting college, the other about to finish (he hopes). People think they must be related to the Romanov Dynasty because their names are Alexandra and Anastasia. What else? He loves teaching. He hates paperwork. He loves writing. He hates pens and pencils. He says he loves contemporary music, but it turns out that he means "the contemporaries of Johann Sebastian Bach." He deserted his faith during college but returned to Christ a dozen years later. If you'd like to find out about his spiritual journey, you can read about it at http://www.leaderu.com/real/ri9801/budziszewski.html.

NOTES

Chapter One

1. From the chapter "Schools Ranked by Category" in *The Princeton Review Guide: The Best 311 Colleges—1999 Edition* (Random House/Princeton Review, 1998).
2. Richard John Neuhaus, "Martyrs, Correct and Incorrect," *First Things: A Monthly Journal of Religion and Public Life* 37 (November 1993), pp. 46-47.

Chapter Two

1. I owe the phrasing of "one What in three Whos" to Norman Geisler's helpful book *Answering Islam* (Grand Rapids, Michigan: Baker, 1993), pp. 2, 267.
2. Rick Rood, "The Truth About Heaven," copyright 1998 by Probe Ministries.
3. Rick Rood, "Is There Really a Hell?" copyright 1998 by Probe Ministries.
4. Professor William P. Alston, "Why I Am a Christian," copyright 1995-1998 by Leadership U.
5. John Gay, "Where I Found Real Fulfillment," copyright 1995 by Campus Crusade for Christ.

Chapter Three

1. J. Gresham Machen, *Christianity and Liberalism*, (Grand Rapids, Michigan: Eerdmans).
2. Thomas Nagel, *The Last Word* (New York: Oxford University Press, 1996), pp. 130-131.
3. The quoted words come from the neo-Darwinian paleontologist George Gaylord Simpson, who wrote, "The meaning of evolution is that man is the result of a purposeless and natural process that did not have us in mind"; George Gaylord Simpson, *The Meaning of Evolution*, rev. ed. (Yale University Press, 1967), pp. 344-345. I'm trying to avoid footnotes in this book, but when the subject of Darwinism comes up, you need to know your sources because people will tell you your facts must be wrong.
4. There is a lot of evidence for *microevolution*—for instance, bird beaks getting larger or smaller over many generations. That's not controversial. Where the evidence falls apart is when we get to *macroevolution*—where bird beaks come from in the first place or how fish turn into frogs.
5. For more helpful advice about dealing with Darwinists, take a look at Phillip Johnson, *Defeating Darwinism by Opening Minds* (Downers Grove, Illinois: InterVarsity, 1997).
6. For a clear presentation of the scientific evidence for intelligent design, see Michael J. Behe, *Darwin's Black Box: The Biochemical Challenge to Evolution* (New York: Free Press, 1996). Professor Behe, a biochemist at Lehigh University, does not claim that science can prove that the Designer was God—only that there had to be a Designer.
7. Richard Lewontin, "Billions and Billions of Demons," *The New York Review of Books*, January 9, 1997. By "constructs" Lewontin means hypotheses, by the "phenomenal" world he means the world as we experience it, by "counterintuitive" he

means contrary to what one would expect, and by "*a priori* adherence" he means making up one's mind to believe something before hearing the evidence.

8. Blaise Pascal, *Pensées,* trans. W. F. Trotter (New York: E.P. Dutton & Co., 1943).
9. James W. Sire, *The Universe Next Door: A Basic World View Catalog,* 3rd edition (Downers Grove: InterVarsity, 1997).
10. G. K. Chesterton, *Orthodoxy* (New York, 1909), chapter 8.
11. Adapted from Doug Groothuis, "Evangelizing New Agers," *Christian Research Journal,* Winter/Spring 1987, page 7; copyright by the Christian Research Institute.

Chapter Four

1. John R. W. Stott, *Basic Christianity,* 2nd edition (Downers Grove: InterVarsity, 1971).
2. C. S. Lewis, *Mere Christianity* (New York: Macmillan, 1952).
3. Peter Kreeft and Ronald K. Tacelli, *Handbook of Christian Apologetics* (Downers Grove: InterVarsity, 1994).
4. Ron Brooks and Norman L. Geisler, *When Skeptics Ask: A Handbook of Christian Evidence* (Grand Rapids: Baker, 1995).

Chapter Five

1. John R. W. Stott, *You Can Trust the Bible* (Grand Rapids: Discovery House, 1991), p. 14.
2. Joy Davidman, *Smoke on the Mountain: An Interpretation of the Ten Commandments* (Philadelphia: Westminster Press, 1953, 1954), p. 108.
3. James W. Sire, *Why Should Anyone Believe Anything at All?* (Downers Grove: InterVarsity, 1994).
4. "Perhaps, as my former colleague Francis Crick suggested, no one should be thought of as alive until about three days after birth. . . . If a child were not declared alive until three days after birth, then all parents could be allowed the choice that only a few are given under the present system." These quotations are from "Children from the Laboratory," *Prism: The Socioeconomic Magazine of the American Medical Association* 1:2 (1973), pp. 12-14, 33-34.
5. NancyJo Mann, as quoted in Christine Russell, "Don't Do This," *Washington Post,* (January 23, 1983), p. A13.
6. Personal communication, February 26, 1996. I thank Professor Plantinga for allowing me to quote from his letter.

Chapter Six

1. Randy Alcorn, *Pro Life Answers to Pro Choice Arguments* (Sisters, Oregon: Multnomah, 1992).
2. "Abstinence More Prevalent Than Bruins May Think," "Sextalk" column, *UCLA Daily Bruin* (November 2, 1995).
3. Glenn T. Stanton, *Why Marriage Matters: Reasons to Believe in Marriage in Postmodern Society* (Colorado Springs: Piñon Press, 1997), pp. 57-69.
4. Clay Brown, "Set Free to Follow Christ: Freedom from Pornography," copyright 1995-1998 by Leadership University.
5. St. Augustine, *Confessions* (New York: Penguin, 1961).

Chapter Seven

1. *Hopwood v. State of Texas,* 861 F.Supp. 551 (1994). The case was heard in the Fifth Circuit Court of Appeals, which handles cases in Texas, Louisiana, and Mississippi.

2. To read more about liberal and conservative myths, see my articles "The Problem with Liberalism" and "The Problem with Conservatism" on the *First Things* magazine website, http://www.firstthings.com.
3. Various versions of this satire have been floating around the internet; original source unknown.
4. "Respecting" means "about," and "establishment of religion" means "official church." The wording also implies that Congress is not allowed to stop states from setting up official state religions, but because of the way the Fourteenth Amendment is interpreted, the states aren't allowed to have official religions either.
5. The case was *Everson v. Board of Education* (1947). In another case, *Lemon v. Kurtzman* (1971), it said that "the line of separation, far from being a 'wall,' is a blurred, indistinct, and variable barrier depending on all the circumstances of a particular relationship."
6. Matthew 5:3 puts it differently—not "blessed are you who are poor," but "blessed are the poor *in spirit*." This isn't an either/or situation. Though some writers stress one passage and some stress the other, the traditional interpretation is that *both* kinds of poor are blessed.
7. Thomas C. Reeves, "Not So Christian America," *First Things* 66 (October 1996), pp. 16-21.

Chapter Eight
1. Neal Donald Walsch, *Conversations with God,* Books 1 (New York: G. P. Putnam's Sons, 1996) and 2 (Charlottesville, Virginia: Hampton Roads Publishing, 1997). These books are not really a conversation with God; it turns out that the author thinks God is himself.
2. Various versions of this list have been floating around the internet; original source unknown.

Chapter Nine
1. James W. Sire, *Scripture Twisting: Twenty Ways the Cults Misread the Bible* (Downers Grove: InterVarsity, 1980).
2. Norman L. Geisler and Ron Rhodes, *When Cultists Ask: A Popular Handbook on Cultic Misinterpretations* (Grand Rapids: Baker, 1997).

Chapter Ten
1. George Gaylord Simpson, *The Meaning of Evolution,* rev. ed. (Yale University Press, 1967), pp. 344-345.
2. Francis J. Beckwith and Gregory Koukl, "A Funny Thing Happened on the Way to the Apocalypse," *Relativism: Feet Firmly Planted in Mid-Air* (Grand Rapids, MI: Baker, 1998), p. 74.

Chapter Eleven
1. *Merriam-Webster Online Dictionary,* http://www.m-w.com/home.htm.
2. Marilyn Adamson, "Where I Found Real Purpose," copyright 1995-1998 by Leadership U.

DISCOVER THE ULTIMATE MANUAL FOR FOLLOWING JESUS.

Walk This Way

People are familiar with instruction manuals.
They know that following the guidelines gets them to their goal.
This book uses the Beatitudes as the instructions for discipleship.
It presents them as the "eight steps" to becoming Jesus' disciple in a fun,
How-to-Stay-Christian-in-College format that is easy to use
and makes discipleship accessible to everyone.

Walk This Way: An Interactive Guide to Following Jesus
(Tim Woodroof) $14

Get your copies today at your local bookstore, visit our website at www.navpress.com,
or call (800) 366-7788 and ask for offer **#2260**.

NAVPRESS
BRINGING TRUTH TO LIFE
www.navpress.com

Prices subject to change.